CHURCH AND WORLD

CHURCH AND WORLD

HANS URS VON BALTHASAR

TRANSLATED BY A. V. LITTLEDALE
WITH ALEXANDER DRU

HERDER AND HERDER

1967
HERDER AND HERDER NEW YORK
232 Madison Avenue, New York 10016

Original edition: *Sponsa Verbi,*
Johannes Verlag, Einsiedeln.

Nihil obstat: Thomas J. Beary, Censor Librorum
Imprimatur: ✠ Robert F. Joyce, Bishop of Burlington
January 7, 1967

Library of Congress Catalog Card Number 67–14141
© 1967 by Herder and Herder, Inc.
Manufactured in the United States

CONTENTS

CHURCH AND WORLD

INTRODUCTION

THE Church, insofar as she is the bride of Christ, remains enshrouded in mystery. Certainly, she is the "People of God," and, as such, in great measure accessible—resembling here the synagogue. The real distinction begins with Mary, in whom the Word was made flesh; with the Eucharist, which is the flesh, by which we are united with God's substance; and with the Holy Spirit, breathed by the risen Son of man into earthen vessels. The Church is a mystery of love, to be approached only with reverence. Many windows have been opened for us to see into the center, but in the most secret chamber the Church remains hidden. In faith we know this, and it is from this standpoint that we are directed to interpret what can be seen of the Church. And if that is so, then the image of the Church which results is likely to be quite different from the current fashionable ones.

1.

THE CONTEMPORARY
EXPERIENCE OF THE CHURCH

THERE is a danger, when one is confronted with the many different "spiritualities" in the Church, in comparing the features of one with the features of another, in an effort to determine which is "best" and which is "worst." These spiritualities include all those which have come and gone in the history of the Church, and also those which remain even today; and from among these spiritualities, of course, one is free to choose according to personal inclination or inner calling. Certainly, freedom as such, and therefore also the freedom of the Christian, has as one of its fundamental characteristics a detachment from circumscribed motives and forms which are merely ephemeral. But this is not the heart of freedom, for freedom consists also in the possibility of deciding for the best, for what appears essential. It consists in identifying oneself, in other words, with the very thing which is chosen in its living and pulsating origin; and, in the strength of this unconditioned reality, in acting on the unformed and confused events of the time, clarifying them and imparting to them a consistent structure. Thus, great movements in the history of the Church have always begun by brushing aside all "spiritual" boundaries—for these tend to separatism and are of themselves insufficiently grounded in reality—and by returning to the original impulse of the Gospel.

To distinguish, therefore, between the extant kinds of spirituality—which nowadays is generally either the spirituality of the various religious Orders and Congregations, or of the secular clergy, or of the laity or groups of lay people—is practically a useless exercise, perhaps well intentioned, but more often than not (and not always unconsciously) tainted with a spirit of animosity. It is as though any one of the saints could have been thus preoccupied with his own special spirituality! This departmentalizing of spirituality, furthermore, is quite out of harmony with the ways of the Holy Spirit, whose only true purpose is to infuse into men's hearts the fullness of Christ, and this fullness permits of no restriction. Therefore, there can be no question of propounding, alongside all the other forms of piety alive in the Church, one special spirituality for the Church of today. To support this idea we must keep in mind that the Church herself is "the fullness of him who fills all in all" (Eph. 1, 23). Indeed, it is the Church who imparts offices and charismata, precisely because Jesus Christ "ascended far above all the heavens, that he might fill all things" (Eph. 4, 10), as a means to "building up the body of Christ, until we all attain . . . the fullness of Christ; so that we may no longer be children, tossed to and fro and carried about with every wind of doctrine . . . but speaking the truth in love, we are to grow up in every way into him who is the head, into Christ" (Eph. 4, 12–15).

In other words, what is needed is an understanding of every particular mission in the Church as proceeding from the whole Church, and destined for the growth and deepening of the life of the whole Church. This understanding can come about in the individual only from a love for the whole Church imparted by the Spirit of unity.

To propound, therefore, a special "modern spirituality" demands an *a priori* theological assumption, or rather—since we do not want to mince matters—a theological prejudice. The ground of this is not a clearly worked-out, personal view, but the Spirit of the wholeness of Christ, who alone can teach us to choose out, from among the bewildering mass of spiritualities now current, what is of real significance, what really matters, since it

12

represents, not what man produces in his own interest, but the Spirit of the Church's fullness. What points the way and conditions our choice is not the "high things" of human ingenuity or originality, but the "humble," which the Spirit enjoins us to concur with (Rom. 12, 16), and which bear the sign of fruitfulness. It is true that the Church's fruitfulness is not an object of direct observation. The source whence it springs lies in the inward, invisible sphere. When it flows outward and produces a visible change, the connection is such that it can only be felt and glimpsed in faith; it can never be established by the methods of ordinary experience. Nonetheless, the Holy Spirit does not leave the Church without some visible, convincing signs, such as the miracles of the saints, especially those of the moral order.

Though we may not make any judgment in respect to good or evil without prejudicing God's judgment, yet we are told to recognize the tree of good and evil by its fruits, spiritual and secular. In practice, this means that while we attend to the signs of our time (to read them is part of our Christian duty), we must look for the signals which sanctity in the Church, canonized or not, has set up for us. It is there that we always find true fruitfulness and therewith the proof that the Holy Spirit intends *this* and not something else, on which, perhaps, much ink and organization is lavished. Unless the Lord build the house, the architects of modern spirituality labor in vain. But the Lord gives sleep to his own, the sleep of peaceful, "abiding" love and contemplation. Therefore, we must listen to the heart's resonance: when our heart is deeply stirred when the Church is spoken of, taking note of the direction towards which it spontaneously turns in inmost hope, where it feels directly touched, not because it has finally been talked into something, but knows itself to be understood prior to any human utterance. It matters little to the heart whether or not the expression which captivates it already has received its final form and precision, if it is even open to misconstruction, a word of various meanings to the many; the Christian heart has itself understood.

If we take this criterion seriously—not in any fanatical or

illuministic fashion, but wholly in the framework of the Catholic Church, in obedience to her, attentive to her heartbeat—there results as if spontaneously, and right at the outset, a great cleavage which allows us at once to throw off half of the material that we supposed we had to carry with us. If we listen to the way the Spirit blows and to *his* signs of the time, listen therefore in a pure attitude of faith and prayer to his directing, then we can say with certainty beforehand: the Spirit of Jesus will, today as always, not give his Church anything other than the Spirit of Jesus himself. Now this means that the spirituality of the Church can, at every time and also in the present, be only spiritual, and not worldly in the sense of desiring earthly power, the power to assert herself with new and promising methods of political, diplomatic, economic, sociological organization, which would assure to the visible Church greater independence, and greater influence in the world. This holds good even if these promising methods are applied primarily internally in order to tighten discipline, to cleanse and lubricate the joints, centralize the direction, assure greater uniformity of utterance and directives, and raise the standards, moral and intellectual, of the clergy and, as far as possible, of the laity. All these are watchwords of integralism, which, as we here understand it, is at the opposite pole to the Spirit which blows when it wills. To this extent, there exist *within* the empirical Church two opposing spirits, such as Augustine describes, following the Bible of the old and the new covenant, as the battle between two *civitates;* and the *Spiritual Exercises* of Ignatius (more spiritually) as the opposition of two casts of mind: on the one hand, the Luciferian, the will to power; on the other, the Christian, the will to poverty, abasement, humility. The worst feature of integralism is that, out of this mentality, which obviously should be most consciously fought against in the Christian (otherwise, why the exercise of the "two banners" in regard to the most inward, secret decision for Christ?), it makes a combined front of the visible Church and the visible non-Church, and for that very reason (since the battle is fought out in the world) claims for

14

the Church the means used by those who do not belong to it.

The program of integralism, however, may claim its appropriate place even within a spiritualized idea of the Church. It is no infallible sign of the Spirit to renounce all hold on worldly positions, all means of propaganda, organization, and centralization, all technical methods of communication and dissemination; and from, it may be, the collapse of all these positions—or, to speak plainly, from Communism—to await a spiritual and eschatological salvation, and only start seriously thinking on Christian lines, as it were, on the far side of the Communist era. Meanwhile, the things mentioned are, at best, only means, and are governed by a "so far as," determined by the Spirit—the Spirit of Jesus Christ. For it is the Holy Spirit's aim to lead the Church "into all truth," the truth he "shall receive from mine," from the treasure of Jesus Christ. *"Hoc sentite in vobis."* To hold that this *sentire* somehow follows of itself on the achievement of the integralist ideal is as illusory as the idea of a Communist regime changing dialectically into one of freedom.

The sword which the Lord demands we should fight with, and which St. Paul fought with all his life, is the sword of the Spirit. And it will be shining and sharp if the life we live is sword-like, clear-cut, so that in it the truth is reflected. It is against this manifestation of the truth alone that the real enemies of the Church are opposed, whereas the enemies of integralism may well be friends of Christ, whose severed ear he puts back and heals. Our ideals in regard to the life of the Church do not constitute spiritualities. When we pray for the Church, we ought to ask ourselves if our prayer fits in with that of Christ for the Church. We bear the superabundant treasure of Christ's glory in earthen vessels, that the superabundance of strength may be ascribed to God, not to us. The life of Christ will be visible in us only if, at all times, his passion unto death is made visible in our life (2 Cor. 4, 7. 10). Like St. Paul, we must be "always delivered unto death," if the true "integrality" of Christ is to be preserved in us. Thus every kind

15

of integralism, open or disguised, is contrary *in principle* to true catholicity, which can only win to itself and comprise all things if it delivers itself up (the real tradition principle), dies like the seed to rise again. The principle of integralism is the wholeness, the freedom from wounds and scars of the beast in Revelation (13, 12. 14). Man today, more than ever before, needs to be on his guard, remembering that all that he can achieve by his own power (and what can he not?) has no part with what "the Spirit speaks to the Churches."

1.

The Church is, of her very nature, a mystery of faith, and this fact has always been present to the consciousness of every epoch of its history. The patristic age lived naïvely in this consciousness, without feeling the need to construct a distinct, self-contained ecclesiology. Man *was* the Church, he stood in the sphere of light and holiness; but reflexion on the Church became necessary when the question of her structure arose. Men first became conscious of this question as they looked at those outside, as they considered the nature of heresy or Judaism; here was a mirror in which they saw, as in a negative, the contours of the Church. It is this unreflexive consciousness that alone explains, after a fashion, what is most difficult to grasp of all the various decisions in the Church's history (though they were, in fact, not conscious decisions): that of infant baptism, more pregnant for the future even than the paradoxical *"In hoc signe vinces"* of the Constantinian era in which the cross, the sign of the divine helplessness, was made the standard behind which the Church marched onto the field of earthly battle. It is easy to understand how, later on—by appealing to tradition as a source of revelation—theologians sought for a primitive justification to legitimize a Christianity which one did not enter by personal decision, but was unconsciously "born into," as one was incorporated by circumcision into the "carnal" people of the promise; it was going to be infinitely difficult not to take this practice as the model for the *opus operatum*.

Closely connected to the practice of infant baptism was the idea that the Church was, primarily, the "manifestation" of the risen Christ, and, therefore, also of his "glory" in the world. It is an idea which for the Alexandrians (later also for the Carolingian Church) suited the militant character of the Church, whether in the spiritual field (in martyrdom) or even in the secular. Constantine's cross was in reality a sign of victory, and it was only gradually that, behind the Church of glory, men came to glimpse the inner mystery of suffering that it hid, becoming increasingly conscious of the contrast between form and content in the Church.

In the high Middle Ages, despite far-reaching sociological changes, the situation was really no different. Even the embittered controversy between the protagonists of pope and emperor remained on the threshold, as regards the theology of the Church, and was restricted to legal rights; it did not touch on the essence of the matter, for thought was still in the pre-reflexive stage. The core of truth was safeguarded by prayers and meditations of contemplative love; the commentaries on the Song of Songs and on Paul and John, whose content was transmitted uninterruptedly from the patristic era to the scholastic, preserved the heart of the mystery. Great art could reproduce the mystery in its imagery, on the basis of an as yet *undisputed aesthetic and religious correspondence between the inward and the outward, mystery and form.* This relationship persisted as long as the question was not consciously raised as to what, in fact, as expressed in ideas, was the content of the mystery, and what was the outward form. At most, one could say that the content was the kingdom of God that had come with Christ, and its manifestation was Christendom, as a visible corporate body set apart from paganism, Judaism, and Islam—*Christendom,* not the "organized Church" of post-Lutheran times. Such a relationship, undefined but strongly impressed on the mind, could be justified from the standpoint of the Gospel, but it is not identical with that suggested by the latter. It includes a cultural component, which nowadays we mistakenly try to elucidate with the catchword "mythical world-view." There is a

definite order of theological ideas, held unreflexively, that stands
in a fruitful and mutual relationship with a definite order of
cultural and philosophical ideas, also held unreflexively. The
first makes use of the second in order to represent a definite
mode of relationship between consciousness and unconscious-
ness, which seems to it just and incontrovertible. Between the
theological mystery of the relationship of Christ and the Church
and the aesthetic mystery of, say, a cathedral, there existed only
an analogy, not an identity, and no one at that time was de-
ceived by it. The analogy, however, held; it spoke, and said
enough to prevent any attempt to press beyond into the domain
of the rational, after the fashion of the Enlightenment. But
what it said were things that have validity only within an aesthetic symbolism in which the kingdom of heaven "expresses"
itself in the holy kingdom of earth, and which to us today, who
lack this sense of symbolism, seems a terrible misconception.
Within such a world system, there is a justification for the Crusades, —which, however looked at from a biblical standpoint,
signify a reversion to the ideas of the Old Testament (itself
the theological place of symbolism). After all, from the Christian standpoint, all the world seems alike. Wolfram von den
Steinen, with his thorough working out of the "Christian myth,"
has rendered to Christians of today an important service by help-
ing them towards a clearer discernment of spirits. Yet to pro-
ject our modern Christian consciousness back into the Middle
Ages, however illuminating they may be, is quite unjust. For
it is only of ourselves that we ought to be thinking when we
contemplate with astonishment, and often with horror, the too
hastily drawn conclusions of aesthetic symbolism.

The situation becomes quite different at the time of the Reformation, when (despite all the courageous attempts of the
"third force") the consciousness of a breach in the heart of
Christendom compelled men to form judgments based on reason. These, like all judgments of the kind, however indispensable, involved tragic losses. For now the spotlight of reflexion
was turned on what survived of the Christianity of former

times, on the undivided visible Church. And this happened in an age when, through the Reformation itself, but equally through the budding natural sciences, the old view of the world was collapsing and a myth was losing its force—and which could only be regained, if ever, through a long and devious process.

In Catholicism, the result was a breach in the Church's teaching. From now on, the central point became the "form" of the Church in the narrow sense: the three functions of the hierarchy, among which could be counted the sacraments and the forms of worship, the disciplinary laws, and theology as the teaching of defined dogma. *But the question whether this form could or should still be seen as the simple expression of the content of the inner ecclesial mystery of the Church, was basically no longer asked.* In fact, it could not be considered profitably in a transition period like the Baroque, where, at one and the same time, the old aesthetic ideas, for instance in art and in traditional thinking, were continued, but were menaced, or even already abandoned, in natural science and the philosophies colored by it (Descartes, Leibniz, the empiricists, Kant). The medieval, non-reflexive aesthetic system of the correspondence between the inner nature of the kingdom of God and its outward appearance had to give way to a stronger sense of tension —because in part the outcome of reflexion—between the organized hierarchical Church as form and the inscrutable central mystery as content. The two had to be bridged, and this was done explicitly by Ignatius Loyola (in his "Rules for Thinking With the Church"), tragically in the death of Thomas More, heroically in the last *Pensées* of Pascal. Against the idea of functionalism, the epoch of Goethe, of idealism and romanticism, with its concept of the organism, harked back to the old world-image, along with Schleiermacher, Sailer, and Möhler right up to Pilgrim's *Physiology of the Church* and their last offshoots in "organic asceticism" and the ecclesiology of the *corpus mysticum*. But the latter conception, as soon as it was used as the key to the entire doctrine on the Church, was seen

19

to be defective of its very nature. *"Corpus"* and "organism" are images whose exaggerated use in connection with the relationship between the inner nature and outward form of the "organized" Church must not be overlooked. Just as we cannot defend the view[1] that the relationship between the external organization of the Church and its internal mystery is adequately expressed by the comparison of that between the body and soul, so we cannot on biblical grounds maintain a disconnection between the two poles (even if only in the Protestant sense). Such a relationship between content and form as was introduced at the Counter-Reformation cannot be vindicated as the intention of the founder of the Church; nor can it be derived from St. Paul's image of the body (Rom. 12; 1 Cor. 12; Eph. 4), in which the differentiation of the "members" cuts right across the distinction of official and unofficial, impersonal and personal, hierarchical and charismatic. The Pauline imagery is needed only to guard against hasty interpretations. If the Church is the "body of Christ," its Head, then individual Christians, considered as parts, are *his* members, and not actually members of the Church, which, if taken by itself, would not be a body but an acephalous torso. It is the "Head," expressly as "raised up," who determines and distributes offices and charismata (Eph. 4, 11. 16), and, therefore, it is the Trinity (*idem Spiritus, idem Dominus, idem Deus,* 1 Cor. 12, 4–6), and not the Church organizing itself. Likewise, the mutual ordering and subordination (which result from the imparted powers and hierarchical offices) in that light is it to be understood "organically"; looked at immanently, everything is "ministerial." The free Christian obeys pope and bishop for the sake of Christ and through his direct relation to Christ. In other words, it is through the *entire* Spirit of Christ, who is also the Spirit of the *entire* Church, that the individual Christian is inserted as a member in the whole, "for it is not by measure that [God] gives the Spirit" (Jn. 3, 34). Otherwise, the New Testament would not be a covenant of freedom.

1. Which retains the medieval system of non-reflexive "mythical" symbolism, restricted to the hierarchy.

Precisely where an undialectical relationship between form and content has become unacceptable, we find, for the first time, an unequivocally spiritual movement within contemporary ecclesiology. Reflexion on the nature of the Church is as alert as ever. On all sides we hear the call for a satisfactory ecclesiology. At the same time, however, we must be on our guard against facile solutions, and keep before our minds the double question: What is, in fact, the inmost essence of the Church, and—if this cannot be expressed in words—what is the form of its manifestation?

The spiritual (esoteric, we may say) medieval doctrine on the Church was that the Church is the bride of Christ, and this was a continuation of the patristic doctrine. The mystery is love, is marriage, in a depth and height of meaning that goes beyond the flesh, without denying it; for the mystery of the flesh is itself a great mystery, particularly in relation to Christ and the Church. This enables us the better to understand the splendor and exuberance characteristic of the language used at that time about the Church. But in the late Middle Ages, the ravaged form of the Church on earth was no longer transparent enough to convey her inner radiance. This was, consequently, assigned to the secret marriage of suffering of the individual mystic with the bridegroom; and finally, to Luther, the countenance of the external office of the Church appeared distorted into a Babylonian mask and caricature.

Something of the personal conception characteristic of the late Middle Ages persisted in the Baroque age (mainly seen in the great figures of John of the Cross, Francis de Sales, Fénelon, and Ignatius), so that the external pomp and hierarchical order could no longer be taken directly as the "manifestation" of the hidden splendor of holiness. A hidden cleavage ran through the spirituality of the *grand siècle,* between the personal inwardness of the individual, and the Church theology formed according to Bellarmine, symptomatically illustrated in the opposition between Bossuet and Fénelon.

Now the problem has forced itself into the open, and the differences demand to be fully explored. So we inquire once again into the inner nature of the Church, and come up, more consciously than did the thinkers of patristic times and the Middle Ages, against the problem of the mystery of the Church as it was at its origin. For that is what we have to embody and express in our Christian life.

But is it, indeed, possible to represent the original and inmost being of the Church, or express it conceptually? Scripture speaks of the bride: this is an image that presupposes an actual subject, contrasted with the bridegroom, though united with him in the mystery of the one flesh. But is the Church such a subject? Or is it not rather the sum of the individual believers who as such are subjects by nature, and not simply through the grace of Christ? Does the splendid imagery of the Song of Songs, which communicated its profound meaning in a non-reflexive mode of thought, still hold good for us moderns? Or perhaps we should, with Karl Barth, demythologize what eludes clear comprehension both in the object and in our consciousness, and revert to a simple encounter between person and person, to the concept of the people of God as found in the Old Testament, the Qumrân scrolls, and Protestantism, —as, to be sure, many among us are now proposing. This means following *The City of God* rather than the *Commentaries on the Psalms*. And it has quite a modern touch about it: the Church with its clear lines like a building designed with all the most up-to-date techniques, all that savors of myth swept away, and the mystery concentrated more or less on the person of Christ, God and man.

We can see at once that this approach is inacceptable, since it means abandoning the core, inapprehensible but essential, of the mystery, to which the words "bride," "body," and "people" can serve only as pointers. The "bride" who, issuing from the wounded side of the new Adam, is at the same time his "body" (and only for that reason his "people") is both the One (with Christ) and the Other (over against him), in a relation at once of independence and freedom for which there is no analogy in the created sphere, but only in the Trinity. The

22

Church is the grace and fullness of Christ poured out into the "other" (created) subject, and is not only act, but also result, yet result never separable from act. For this reason, the "bride" can never desire to think of herself as definitively "over against" her Lord, but only as pressing on to closer union with him, the source of her being. There can be no ecclesiology which is not, at its core, Christology; and if it is to proceed on the right lines, it must begin by renouncing itself. Its unity is not a second unity next to the unity of Christ: this is true of its totality of body and spirit. For this reason, the nuptial mystery of the "one flesh" can only be a simile for it, just as Eve's coming forth from Adam's side is no more than a simile, even though we take it that her soul, too, came from him. This, however, would stretch the biblical image into a Christological one, and still remain imperfect in its new application. But if Christ is the incarnation of the God who rightly bears the name of *"Non-aliud"* (see Nicholas of Cusa)—precisely because he is the Wholly Other!—, then he cannot be the "One" to whom the Church could be contrasted as the "Other." The Church so understood will ultimately be unable to be an object to herself, but will see herself only as the outflowing love of the Lord (and, through him, of the Trinity), and, therefore, as the love flowing out over the world for her redemption. And however conscious she may be of being a continuous expression of gratitude, of responding and confessing in faith, she will understand this not as her own independent action, but as joining in with the Son's *eucharistia* and *confessio* to the Father in their common Spirit. What she can do of herself is as ordinary and insignificant as the portion of bread and wine which disappears by being transsubstantiated into her Lord.

Many consequences follow from this fact, one of them being a new ecclesiological conception of marriage,[1] which only now

1. The biblical exaltation of marriage, in point of fact, rests on (1) the "acephalous" character of woman in contrast to man (not, then, on the two-person relationship), and (2) the mystery of woman's origin from man, which can hardly be considered "retracted" by 1 Corinthians 11, 11–12 (Ephesians 5 was written later).

attains its full theological significance. Another is a new conception of virginity, which is at last being freed from any suspicion of a Gnostic depreciation of the body, and is seen as a heightening, rather than a diminishing, of the individual sacrament of marriage, —being a direct participation in the general sacrament which is the mystery of the nuptial fruitfulness between Christ and the Church. For the exaltation of Christian marriage is always accompanied by that of Christian virginity. Another consequence is a new consciousness of the Church as servant; for the mystery of her own bridal relationship is not her own appurtenance, but is wholly in the Lord, in the depths of his being; and the Church, in whatever aspect she comes to view herself, can only see herself as the handmaid of the Lord. In this we have, undoubtedly, the key to the present interest in Mariology. It is as if the Church, in striving after self-knowledge, were more and more insistently confronted by God with this particular mirror, the bride without spot or wrinkle, ignorant of self-reflexion, knowing herself solely as handmaid, however much she be the woman crowned with the sun, moon, and stars, the queen of heaven. In Mary the Church can look upon herself without risk of confusion; not only because she can never identify herself with Mary (for, in concrete, it is always sinners who contemplate her), but because what she sees in Mary is always the opposite of identification. Only at the end of time can she hope to reach the level of her most exalted member, when the stain of original sin shall have been washed away, virginal integrity restored, bodily assumption into heaven completed. Till then, the Church, in honoring Mary, cannot be honoring herself, and the more she (as the Church triumphant being gathered into heaven) comes to resemble her archetype, the less liable will she be to the temptation. Anyone who clearly understands this dialectic can easily combine a tender and ardent devotion to Mary with all the contemporary warnings against Mariological exaggerations, since these are the fruit of a radical misunderstanding of the Marian principle. Mary herself had neither the vocation nor the inclination to concern herself with Mariology, and neither has the Church to construct an ecclesiology that goes beyond an outline or even beyond guarding against error or explaining her own transcendence. And just as no Christian should indulge in the contemplation of his own (infused or acquired) virtues, still less may his holy mother, the hierarchical Church, do so, for it is from her Spirit that he acquires his own spirit of humility and modesty. But if the Church, as the handmaid of the Lord, may not glorify herself, yet it does not become her sons to besmirch her earthly crowns which she does not know what to make of in this period of history. It is not without significance that, as has often been remarked, the Marian definitions and those of the First Vatican Council on the place of Peter occurred at the same period; they each support the other, and elucidate their real purpose. They do so, however, only when considered in the Spirit of Christ and as the expression of his Spirit, and are not used as a vehicle for the self-glorification of the Church, internal and external, in an earthly integralistic sense. The Marian spirit of unity with the Lord, in her virginal body and in obedience, is also the Petrine spirit of an unreflexive ecclesial obedience for the sake of the Lord and his nuptial mystery, obedience even to the cross. It is a spirit of surrender without thought of self, which, in both cases—the *Mater Dolorosa* and the crucified Peter—reaches the point of complete acceptance.

At this same point there appear, moreover, all those spiritual impulses, apparently extraneous to all the traditional social forms of the Church, and desirous of drawing their sustenance directly from the Lord, which are expressly not concerned with bringing the "Church" to the world, but solely the Lord and *his* love. Typical of many cases is that of Charles de Foucauld, who cut himself off externally, spatially, more and more from any visible connection with the Church, so as to be alone in the desert, among savage tribes, like an embodied essence of the Church, standing before the Eucharistic Lord, and letting his outpourings of grace stream through him. Then, posthumously in his sons and daughters, he sought out the most hopeless and

25

unpromising places, with the express intention of bringing nothing to the world, neither school nor medical help, nor anything
to do with culture, but only the humble love of the Lord. "Ceaselessly," he makes the Lord say, "must you descend, ceaselessly
humble yourselves, ceaselessly must the first take the lowest
place, in the spirit of humility, in the desire to serve." —
"Work for the sanctification of the world, work at it like my
mother, without speaking, in silence. Build your dwellings
among those who do not know me, bring me into their midst
by erecting there an altar, a tabernacle, and bring there the
Gospel, not by word of mouth but by example, not by preaching
but by living it." — "Example is the sole external work by
which one can influence souls whose attitude to Christ is one of
complete rejection."—"Our hearts must be quite poor, emptied,
void, free, detached from all that is not God and Christ, in order to be rich and overflowing with his love, filled with his love,
captured by his love, depending on him alone."

For Charles de Foucauld, the Church is no longer an object
for contemplation, but wholly gathered up in her act of worship, in which she becomes the channel for the all-uniting love
of Christ. Something analogous might be said of the standpoint
and action of other groups and movements, which do not so
much lead to the Church and illuminate the way, as they try,
simply, to be the illuminating spirit of the Church: ". . . blameless and innocent, children of God without blemish in the midst
of a crooked and perverse generation, among whom you shine
as lights in the world" (Phil. 2, 15). In these cases, *sentire cum
Ecclesia* is raised to a higher plane, that of *sentire Ecclesiae*. This
is only possible in complete self-abnegation and obedience to
the hierarchy, as we have seen already in connection with the
spiritual unity of the Marian and Petrine aspects. This will
always be the guarantee of their purity and genuineness.

From this it may be seen that it is not due to the influence
of contemporary "realism," but to a sense of what is real in the
sacred sphere, that we are more and more losing all taste for
the pomp and circumstance designed to impress man with the

majesty of the Church. There is, simultaneously, an increasing trend towards simplicity ("associate with the lowly," Rom. 12, 16), towards awareness of the lowliness of all the elements of the Church which emphasize her function as servant. "Prestige" is no longer to be sought by outward display, —and the idea that the Church could acquire prestige by such means has been finally quashed by Georges Bernanos. It is now clear to everyone that—if we must speak still of prestige—the Church will gain more in the eyes of men the less she concerns herself with it, and the more obedient she is to the Lord's injunctions to his disciples. In this connection it may be affirmed, not as a daring conjecture, but as a simple fact, that even the numerous canonizations make comparatively little impression on the faithful, as does everything, in fact, which can be effected by organizational machinery. The faithful are impressed, not by canonization, but by sanctity, and mostly by those who, without human striving and human means, are pointed to directly by the Holy Spirit and by him brought into prominence. We are not here objecting to the canonization process as such. But it is today the tacit desire of men that canonization be, above all, a manifestation of sanctity, the mother calling attention to the conduct of this or that fellow saint; an act, then, of the Church obedient and serving rather than self-glorifying. Nowhere so much as here is quantity the enemy of quality.

In our day, of course, there is discernible in all quarters a certain bit of animosity towards papal centralism, an animosity which often misses the point, and is pardonable at most on human grounds, but not on Christian ones. Examined closely, however, this unrest is not always basically a refusal *sentire cum Ecclesia,* but more often the expression of a deep conviction that the hierarchy has indeed a sacral function for the Church, but that this function is wholly one of service. This hierarchy is the crystallization of the love of the Lord who established it as necessary for this sinful world (most necessary, in fact, when it accepts the humble task of instructing and exacting obedience in the name of the Lord). As soon as this attitude is recognized,

27

many a fault-finder is prepared for joyful coöperation. The spirituality of the hierarchy remains to this day indirectly formed and burdened by a forceful theology of the late primitive Church, the "ecclesiastical hierarchy" of Denis the Areopagite which, unconcerned with the actuality of sin, was content to portray an ideal Church, a Church as she ought to be. This theology identified office with sanctity, the higher office with the higher sanctity, the transparency of the official function with the transparency of contemplation rapt in its sacred object. This ideal surely must be an inspiration to the members of the hierarchy; but precisely for that reason it may not encourage substitution or compensation for deficient personal holiness by the objective holiness of office (as the Areopagite was sometimes consciously or unconsciously interpreted during the Middle Ages and later). The office is no less sacred to the faithful of today than it was to former generations, but it is now soberly regarded as the means to actual sanctity, and as the holier and more venerable the more clearly it represents the kenosis of Christ.

A final consequence follows. The hierarchy is no longer seen merely as the "manifesting corpus," the embodiment of the Church's intrinsic, mysterious, holy status of bride, but rather as a serving office which is to transform this original hidden holiness into an external holiness of life and love, —and there has been a corresponding change in apologetics. The *notae Ecclesiae*—closely connected with the hierarchy—of fundamental theology now lose some of their forcefulness in favor of the pivotal *nota* of holiness. "By this shall all men know that you are my disciples, that you love one another" —this, surely, is *the* apologetic of Christ and the apostles. The unity of Christians, so strongly emphasized in the high-priestly prayer, is surely not of human making, but a Trinitarian gift; and it can be nothing other than the expression and manifestation of this supernatural love. *"Ubi peccata sunt, ibi est multitudo, ibi schismata, ibi haereses, ibi dissensiones; ubi autem virtus, ibi singularitas, ibi unio, ex quo omnium credentium erat cor unum et anima una"* (Origen). It is *this* unity—and not one allegedly exacted by the power of the keys—, it is *this* catholicity and apostolicity which can bring about apostolic effects. It might, for instance, lead a Newman from the Anglican *via media* into the Catholic Church.

All these aspects are interrelated. They follow easily once the principle from which they rise has been grasped. The fact that their multiplicity can be brought to unity may well indicate that we have accurately touched on the principle of which they are the expression.

2.

A further conclusion can be drawn from the above. If the Church and the individual Christian are worthy of belief, and impress by the fact that they do not point to themselves but are suffused by and show forth Christ's love, if the Church and the Christian alone can capture the world's attention by proclaiming something other than themselves, then this self-abnegation in the service of Christ is clearly the only possible way of revealing to the world the self-abnegation of Christ. This kenosis of Christ, consummated in the death on the cross, is the very point of origin of the Church and Christian as such. It is the point of the incomprehensible generative power of Christ, who bears the entire Church within himself. She exists nowhere else but within him (and, ultimately, the entire hope, the entire faith of the old covenant spring from thence). As Christ has received from the Father the power to surrender his life, as he breathes forth his spirit on the cross in an extremity of weakness, so he can also, at Easter, breathe his Spirit into the Church. His weakness unto death is his divine and his human power, his omnipotence, willing assume the form of utter powerlessness.

The Church and the Christian are, undoubtedly, products of this unique generative power on the cross. This does not mean, however, that, as products, they are ever separable from the act by which they originated. " 'As the Father has sent me, even so I send you.' And when he had said this, he breathed on them, and said to them, 'Receive the Holy Spirit' " (Jn. 20, 21–22).

It is the Spirit who wills to be continually breathed forth, and who, for that reason, must be ever anew breathed forth from a principle which is both Trinitarian and Christological. Ecclesial piety today is more closely bound up than ever before with this mystery. The Church community is the true product of the solitude of Christ, his solitude on the cross, his solitude as the incomparable God-man, which is, in turn, the manifestation of his Trinitarian solitude, and ultimately of the primordial solitude of the Father in the generation of the Son. The Christological solitude is the active source of all Christian Church-community. The Christian must be not only Church generated, but the Church co-generating, regenerating: he must be the Church in origin, the Church in solitude. This is solitude which evokes community, apostolic solitude which does not go out from the Church, but in which the Church herself goes out into the world. It is not private, existentialist solitude, for it is most profound community in and with Christ, just as Christ's solitude is always—even in his dereliction on the cross—community in and with the Father. But such solitude in origin can become so abysmal as to occlude the experience of community. The Church is the pure outpouring of the Lord; the Christian the pure outpouring of Christ and Church. The Christian proceeds from community with Christ, from community with Church. Bearing this duplex community he advances towards a community to be regenerated: but he goes his way in solitude. It is ultimately the solitude of the generating Father, the Father who is such only in relation to the Son.

It does not really matter whether this solitude is realized mainly by way of contemplation or by way of the active apostolate. The Carmel is solitude in God, solitude whose meaning is generation of the Church through the Church. In accord with the tradition of her Order, Thérèse of Lisieux used to describe the function of the Carmelite nuns as "mothers of souls." The lifework of John of the Cross was solitary in this most profound sense, in the midst of the Church, as the Church. The celebrated prayer of the Carmelite Elizabeth of the Trinity ("*O mon Dieu,*

Trinité que j'adore"), on which the Benedictine Dom Vandeur has written so profound a commentary, is a pure prayer of solitude which never mentions the Church at all, for it is a prayer from the very heart of the Church. For example, Edith Stein's commentary on John of the Cross, *The Science of the Cross,* leads to the same conclusion. This agreement among the great Orders (to which may be added, as representative of all the rest, Francis of Assisi and Antony of the Desert) is significant in that they all take as their starting point the sending of disciples into the world. If the movement of the synagogue and of Israel is always centripetal (*"habitare fratres in unum"*), that of the Church—from the unity of the Church—is centrifugal (*"ite in universum mundum"*). Even the autarchic abbey does not escape this law, which makes it a city set on a mountain, radiating a light which directs others to their end. The "community life" of the Orders is an instrument for the self-abnegation and apostolic solitude of the individual, exercising them in renunciation of self and Christian love. *"Vita communis maxima poenitentia,"* as John Berchmans said.

This explains the missionary spirituality of the "secular institute," whose members, as a rule, have to go singly through the world, endowed with the strength of the Church-community, and carrying it into realms alien to the Church. Certainly, they have to be sowers and planters of a new Christian community, not to dwell there in comfort, but to continue their journeying from there as apostles in a new solitude. It is obvious that this spirituality as a form of life is not for everyone, but it belongs, in however attenuated a degree, to the ecclesial maturity and responsibility of those who have been confirmed. One cannot be simply—today less than ever—the Church as a product; one must always be the Church producing. The Church-community can never be definitively rounded off and self-contained; once it has reached this stage it must open out in the *"Ite, missa est"* to the world and to solitude.

This raises the problem of the liturgy, which today more than ever agitates the Church as a whole. The problem consists, in the first place, in recovering what is genuine and real from the accumulations of the centuries. In reaction against the untenable liberalism of making liturgy a personal matter, we must make every effort to arouse the sense of community within the liturgy, to restore liturgy to the ecclesial plane, where individuals can take their proper place in it. On this plane they must learn to be the holy people set apart, instead of individuals. Liturgical piety involves a total turning from concern with one's inner state and self-abnegation to the attitude and feeling of the Church. It means enlarging the scope of prayer, so often narrow and selfish, to embrace the concerns of the whole Church and, indeed—as in the "Our Father"—of God himself. In fact, this violent, this often "crucifying" sacrifice of the pious subject to the ecclesial object (this is what Schleiermacher and Hegel call "community-consciousness") is, ultimately, one of the conditions for the presence of the Eucharistic Lord: "Where two or three are gathered together..."—that is, where individuals, in profound faith and obedience, desire to be and to realize the Church—"there I am in the midst of you."

Nonetheless, despite what enthusiasts for the liturgical movement often seem to think, liturgical piety does not replace personal prayer, the encounter of the soul with God in the intimacy of the Sermon on the Mount. Community prayer calls, in fact, for personal contemplative prayer, which becomes by that fact ecclesial prayer. When the liturgy seems not to tolerate contemplation within itself and alongside itself—especially through a busy activism; for example, when the sacred action of the altar is accompanied by the roar of loudspeakers and other machinations which make private prayer impossible—then it degenerates into a worldly thing. The Christian ought to come away from the liturgical sacrifice not with the satisfied sense of having accomplished something, but inwardly strengthened, and with the ardent desire, in the words of so many post-communions, to realize in his life what has just been sacramentally enacted. This integration of community and individual prayer has certainly begun in our time, but it is not yet well enough understood, nor approached from both directions. We yet lack adequate directives. To supply these, the older Orders, whose merit it is to have abetted the liturgical revival in various regions, need only recall their own ancient tradition (as has been done for the Middle Ages by Dom Jean Leclerq in his excellent book *The Love of Learning and the Desire for God*). In this way they can recall to life the synthesis already present in the Church, avoid the dangers and by-products of a too exterior liturgism, without foregoing anything of value already acquired. In the absence of real, personal contemplation concurrent with the liturgy, and if the cultivation of community-consciousness is not accompanied by the building up of the Christian person, then his sense of himself as externally representing the Church is illusion. The unity into which he merges himself would then be simply that of a pious group-consciousness after the Protestant manner, and not ecclesial community-consciousness aglow with fervor, whose direct source is the bridegroom, Christ.

The axis of this ecclesial community-consciousness is the redemptive love of Christ which he imparts without diminution or compromise to his bride. To know the real spirit of this consciousness, we have only to recall the evangelical counsels by which Christ prepares—for those who desire it—the way to the mystery of the cross. The counsel of virginity, —for the Church is virginal in the core of her sentiments (2 Cor. 11, 2); the counsel of poverty in spirit and reality, —for the Church is poor in all that is her own in order to be a receptacle for the fullness of Christ; the counsel of utter docility, —for the Church, as body and bride, must necessarily be at the disposal of the bridegroom. Thus it is that our generation begins to perceive that the evangelical counsels concern each believer who desires to attune his own heart to the pulse of the Church, not only in an objective performance of the cult-mystery, but in the *leiturgia,* the service of his whole life. And since the counsels of Christ are the key to his own crucified love (and there is no other than his), then, according to 1 Corinthians 7, 29–31, they pertain to every state in the Church, and must be observed by each.

Sentire cum consiliis (if these are properly understood in Christ's sense) is identical with *sentire cum Ecclesia.* We have to rid ourselves of the superficial idea of an opposition between the two forms of the Christian life, an idea which comes from considering only how the different states of life diverge, instead of going back further to their underlying unity. For, unless this is done, how is it possible to understand what is meant by "the mind of the Church"? For example, if anyone constructs a spirituality of the lay state and of marriage from the standpoint of its distinction from the religious and priestly state, he is thereby debarred from perceiving what lies at the root of both, the spirituality of the Church as such. And it is the same, too, if he assigns the "secular state" to the temporal sphere and the duties pertaining to the kingdom of God in the world, and the "religious state" to the new eschatological age. In so doing, he somehow presumes a split in the Church, whether he intends to or not. But the Church, as a single *totality,* has on principle died to the world with Christ and with him ascended into heaven, to be sent forth from thence into the whole world. Thus the Church is bound as a single totality to Christ's entire redemptive act, and the divergent ways of marriage and virginity must be the expression of this totality.

This reference to the common root of the states of life is of great practical importance for the secular institutes. Insofar as the secular institutes understand to the core their own thought, and can *live* it (and this is not always the case), insofar as they are capable of bringing their thought to the attention of the external Church (and this has barely been indicated), —to this extent are they called, if not to clear away the sterile dualism of the states of life in the Church, then at least to lessen it considerably, and to bestow on the apostolic essence of the states of life a virtually primitive-Christian newness. The Christian layman or lay woman who lives a life of celibacy, poverty, and disponibility, purely for the love of Christ, presents a far greater challenge to the non-Christian and Christian world than does the member of a religious Order, who essentially lives a well-organized and somewhat sheltered traditional life. The member of the secular institute does not preach, but his very life is a positive and abiding witness to the presence of the Church in the world. He is in privileged, if certainly not in exclusive fashion, the Church manifest, the sign of proclamation not of himself but of the Church and of Christ. More precisely, he is a member of Christ manifest, and membership necessarily refers to the body. This is manifestation: and it is not for the common multitude but for those individuals who can withstand the perils of witness by virtue of their mission and their fidelity to this mission. This is manifestation: and it implies being prepared for frustration, being prepared to see an entire effort (such as that of the priest-workers) fail the first time, and to revoke that effort without for all that considering it completed, settled. In the case of the priest-workers it was clearly a question of overcoming a bourgeois prejudice against the priesthood as such, whose civil status was called into question. Objectively, there is no reason why the witness of the ordained Christian should be more important, more meritorious, more conspicuous, more precious than that of the layman; *a priori,* the reverse ought to be expected. On account of anticlerical prejudice, the experiment with priests appears more productive of both gain and loss, and yet both the gains and the losses may have helped to dispel some of the prejudice. Those lay people who will remain in the forefront of controversy will be less in the limelight, but their witness as Church in the most worldly world will be no less effective. If they have chosen, in addition, to heed the evangelical counsels, they can the more forcefully embody the radical unity of the Church, overcoming the world, without fleeing it, by the power of self-denying love.

The example of such a life must react, and already does react upon the married state and on the priesthood and on the old Orders and Congregations: on the married state by inspiring the realization of the counsels; on the priesthood by suggesting a more radical interpretation of the apostolate in the spirit of the Gospels; on the religious state by emphasizing the fact that even in its traditional form, this state interiorly no less is, no less must be the manifestation of the Church than are her exterior manifestations. In each case the central concern is the Church, and not the specific ways of life, old or new. In each case it is a question of renouncing fruitless comparisons, in favor of a deep personal awareness of Church. In each case it is a question of submitting personal piety to the focal point of ecclesial awareness. This awareness does not lie in political or cultural spheres, but unequivocally in the origin of the Church in Christ, an origin which can altogether be perceived only in faith and love, and in the spirit of resolute discipleship.

The Church, then, must be conceived of as having her center not within herself, as an external, worldly organization, but outside herself, in Christ who engenders her. From this it can be seen that the Church, while inwardly reaching out to the Lord, must for that very reason externally go out beyond herself into the world. Hence the characteristic which Friedrich Heer so strongly insists upon, that ecclesial love must, in its Christo-logical core, be love for one's enemies, love and turning towards the non-Christian brother without, —if in this perspective there can indeed still be a "without" in any real sense. If the Church is understood as dynamic in her very origin, as the irradiation of Christ into the world to be redeemed, then the world itself, into which she radiates, is her proper and natural sphere. On this account, the Church must have a worldly form, spatial and institutional: sacrament, hierarchy, and dogma. The non-Christian world may indeed judge her by what is institutional in her, and even her own sinful element may, for the sake of convenience and as a means of escape, cling to these institu-tional elements. But this does not mean that the Church in her true nature, the holy Church, has to interpret herself in this way. On the contrary, she will understand the unchangeable "bone structure" given in her foundation, in the light of its function in the living organism, whose life and activity are guaranteed by this very structure. We cannot say of any living thing that there is a "tension in unity" between the bone structure and the flesh: still less can we say so of the supernatural image of Christ, the Church, in whom everything, however conditioned by her situation in the world, is to be understood as the crystallization of the love of Christ. Seeing and recognizing this at all times was the art of the saints, and it is the same now as always. Love of one's enemies as the axial element—and not just as an incidental act of heroism—is Christian *agapē* in the form appropriate for our time. It would not be itself were it viewed simply as a relation between members of the Church, an interchange between those already in a state of charity towards one another. Certainly, it is entirely in accord with the synoptic, the Pauline, and the Johannine teachings that the mutual love of Christians be a light in the world, drawing attention to itself, —that is, to Christ, the source of this light. But this simply means that love within the Church must not be closed in on herself, but must have a far-reaching apostolic and redemptive significance for the world, as is seen today mainly in the much discussed idea of the whole world as a single family.

One further observation on this point. Once the Church is understood in this twofold transcendence in relation to the Lord and to the world, a new kind of love for her is enkindled, a love that is far more tender and devoted than any enthusiasm which might be enkindled by her visible structure. It is impossible to avoid an impression of fanaticism and narrow-mindedness as long as the Church strives for prestige or for preponderance, and as long as the motive force is not love for the hidden central mystery of the Church and the urge to defend it in the external sphere. But the burning love of the Christian for this profound mystery is itself a mystery. If we think of the Church primarily in contradistinction to the Lord, as a corporation endowed with graces and the means to grace, the faithful, as members of the Church, will surely not refuse homage, admiration, and loyalty, love and obedience, today any more than before. For it is she who "has" the Holy Spirit of Christ, and from her the individual obtains a participation in this Spirit, who, therefore, is always the Spirit of the Church.

But is this way of looking at the Church adequate? Does it not envisage merely a partial aspect, which should never be divorced from the primordial mystery that is never fully revealed? For the mystery is not disclosed (since it is ultimately to be seen in the light of the mystery of the Trinity) as to how far the actual reality of the Church is in Christ (even where she presents herself as his fullness), and how far she is in contradiction to Christ (that is, as a reality engendered by his creative power). For this reason, it can never be finally settled whether the Christian only "believes the Church" or, at the same time, "believes in the Church." He believes her only insofar as she is the emanation of the fullness of Christ, who is God: and only God can one believe. This being so, then also is the Christian's love towards the Church not simply love directed to an entity apart in itself, but, most certainly, love which only begins with the Church in order to become love for Christ and God, a transparent and transitive love, which, as such, is ultimately the love of the Church for her Lord and bridegroom. Devotion to the Church in the present age will be, at its core, not love towards the Church, but love which is that of the Church.

Identification of one's own life with the inmost center of the Church, where she is simply the bride in the presence of the bridegroom, is the ultimate and abiding justification of the contemplative life. No doubt, this can be adjusted to the time in its varying details, not only in the mitigation of its observances, but, perhaps mainly, in a more radical, more consequential ecclesiological form of piety. Nonetheless, the paradoxical fact of its power of attraction shows how wrong they are who consider contemplation outdated or tolerate, at most, the *contemplativus in actione*. Mary of Bethany can never be dispensed with. *Personam Ecclesiae gerit:* she represents, in her special role, the Church herself. She actualizes in the world of human consciousness the inmost mystery of the nuptials between Christ and the Church, God and the world, grace and nature, a relation that is the mystery both of Mary's fecundity as mother and of that of the Church. It is a mystery which, in its absolute finality in itself, and in its "unconcernedness," is itself the focal point, just as, Song of Songs, in the love between bride and bridegroom is fulfilled in itself, is sufficient in its inner fecundity, without procreation, without any further action. That the contemplative life in the Church is also a life of penitence and mortification, a crucified life as well as a marriage festivity, is simply the final consequence, as the Church has always understood it and still today is given to understand it through the inspiration of the Holy Spirit.

3.

The transitive character of present-day devotion to the Church has one final characteristic, inasmuch as the "world" that confronts the Church is not merely an undifferentiated world (though, in principle, redeemed by the Lord of the Church), but, to a great extent, is a Christian world, or the "non-Catholic Church." Everyone nowadays is aware of what this involves, and so we can state it briefly. We feel the cleavage in Christendom much more deeply than men did in the centuries since the Reformation—not only in the West, but, increasingly, between East and West—and feel it as something whose guilt we all share, as inexcusable, and as a most evident obstacle to the Church's apostolic work. For us the schism is the outward indication, the irruption of a long-standing disease in Christendom. However helpless we feel in the presence of the suppurating sore—since, ultimately, it is only individuals who can come to an understanding, and the organized and opposed bodies only with great difficulty—yet we know one thing: that healing, if it is possible, can only come from the power within, from a renewal of love. The source of this love can only be the heart of Christ, and the form it takes will be preëminently that of fervent prayer, prayer for inner unity and outward reunion. It is a love that does not shift all responsibility for action onto the Lord, but works along with him, doing all that can be done in the spirit of the Church, which, essentially, will follow along the lines we have sketched out in the first and second sections; that is to say, it will relate all that pertains to the inner sphere of the Church to its supra-temporal, ever-present point of origin. If all this takes place within the two Christian communities in the course of their self-questioning and in the true spirit of faith, it cannot fail to resolve, in the end, the oppositions inherited from history. There cannot be two ecclesial truths. At the most, it is possible that different aspects come together and complete one another in the one truth; that a partial truth should sink into the background and be almost forgotten in the one comprehensive aspect; that the perspective of the whole should be lost or obscured in a partial view. If Christians of different confessions were, in mutual love, to posit the true act of faith (which always envisages that total Christian truth) —and this, if they believe and love, they are bound to do—then the love of Christ can certainly work in them many a miracle of *rapprochement* and reconciliation.

However, even this aspect of devotion to the Church has its dangers: for it is constantly liable to go to one of two opposite extremes; and so, when Christian love is ardent but insufficiently enlightened, there is need for supervision by the Church. Yet the love that embraces both the Church and other Christian confessions with special intimacy provides, to a great extent, its own safeguards. It knows that differences in doctrine are not unimportant, and that they are not to be glossed over by a liberal approach that ignores or diplomatically minimizes them. They can only be overcome by great efforts on each side to see what in its own position is a cause of separation and of the other's defects, and so bring the two together. Associations for work and discussion between theologians of different confessions are multiplying; they examine, in a new spirit of love and responsibility, both what they hold in common and what separates them. What is most fruitful so far as immediate results are concerned is present-day biblical scholarship, where both sides now work together practically without friction. If this continues long enough, we may have every hope for a *rap-prochement* even in the sphere of dogmatic theology. Certainly, the agreement reached in the last decades on matters of biblical scholarship, even of biblical theology, is unprecedented in the history of the Church since the Reformation. It makes it seem quite out of the question to revert to the usual methods of controversial theology, which ignore the results achieved by biblical scholarship. It is in the joint hearing of God's word that we must let ourselves be jointly instructed on the unity of this word. The Catholic Church has nothing to fear or to lose thereby. It cannot be afraid of any genuine result, even though it may, under the guidance of the Holy Spirit, have to take account of new depths and bolder heights. The harvest to be reaped from the study of the Bible on all levels, from strict scholarship to that of vulgarization, is of immeasurable importance for an understanding of the Church. Here, too, the Christian consciousness is becoming greatly enlarged and open to the full import of revelation, and the Church is thereby attaining a new self-awareness. In addition, we are recovering dimensions which were present to the Middle Ages but lost to view in the religious controversies—that, for instance, of the Augustinian City of God, which comprises both Testaments. The value of the Old Testament in theological controversy is particularly great, since it affords scarcely any occasion for differences of opinion.

And now, for the first time in the Church's history since the days of Justin, the way is opened for communication between the Church and Judaism. The first dialogue, began during the Enlightenment between enlightened Judaism and liberal Protestantism, was of little ecclesiastical significance. The new dialogue, however, which has gradually to forge a way through unforeseeable obstacles, is bound to produce results. It must be conducted in view of the New Testament origins made clear through biblical studies, that is, at the point when the Church actually came into being in history, and from which her being can never be disconnected. It may be that this aspect has not yet penetrated the consciousness of the Church, and that paving the way for dialogue is still seen as a duty of reparation rather than something demanded by the present age of the Church. But if today we are everywhere concerned to gain a clear view of the ecclesial fundamentals and of what the divine intention was regarding the Church, surely the eternal situation described in Romans 9–11 as the primary one in Church and world history must be seen as more urgent and compelling than ever. The matter is far more than one of vague, human sympathy for the new state of Israel, the boldness of its experiment, the courage of its inhabitants. Nor is it merely one of that mutual rivalry between "Jews and Gentiles" through which, according to Paul, God prepares both for his kingdom. It is, ultimately, what concerned the burning love of Paul, his "great sorrow and unceasing anguish," his desire to be "cut off from Christ for the sake of my brethren, my kinsmen by race. . . . To them belong the sonship, the glory, the covenants, the giving of the law, the worship, and the promises" (Rom. 9, 2–4). It concerns the wound that goes so deep into the heart of Paul and the apostles, Christ and the Church, the Lord's weeping over Jerusalem, and his own "anathematization" as the embodiment of (in the first place Israel's) sin. It concerns the ever-present thorn in the Church's flesh, the constant presence of the cross, the guilt of which it is only too easy (as Christian tradition has done) to turn over to the Jews. Admittedly, the Church is not the Lord. She has no power over world history, and her service as spouse is her unconditional agreement with the "inscrutability of his counsels." Yet this expression escapes Paul only when he speaks of the common disobedience of the "Jews and the Gentiles," of God's mercy equally accorded to both, and of the eschatological salvation of Israel. What a close community of destiny is theirs, and what thanks is due from the Church of the Gentiles to Israel thus brought low! The Church begins to form some idea of it in her reading and study of Scripture, seeing how her daily office, the psalms, the prophets, the sapiential books are not only inspired from above, but spring

42

from within the heart of the devout Israel led by the Holy Spirit. "If I forget thee, Jerusalem . . ." It is an inward, indissoluble unity of destiny such as existed between the beloved Jacob and the unloved Esau (Mal. 1, 2–4 = Rom. 9, 13), who draw together while still in the fear of their estrangement: Jacob "went on before them, bowing himself to the ground seven times, until he came near to his brother. But Esau ran to meet him, and embraced him, and fell on his neck and kissed him, and they wept" (Gen. 33, 3–4).

The great, sweeping eschatological views of Romans 11 has been given us for a purpose; it implies certain ethical demands. As a result of it, and of God's victory over the cleft in the heart of Paul and of Christ and the Church, there arises in the consciousness of the Church a tremendous hope and love; so that the deepest source of love springs up from the chasm of the darkest tragedy of world history. Present-day devotion to the Church is dominated by the idea of the collapse of all that divides, the dismantling of the old fortifications. This by no means implies overrunning the eschatological boundaries that have been laid down. What it does imply is obedience to the enjoined meditation on the biblical revelation, its prophetic and dialectical utterance, and its messianic hope of a final synthesis. It is by hope that the seriousness of the dialectic can be measured, a hope that is not without fear, but in which grace superabounds (Rom. 5, 15–21). It is from the horizons thus opened up that the Christian today derives all his confidence and parrhesia. It is as if, in his darkness, this new light is something owed to him; as if the Church, more closely bound to the cross, can thereby obtain a deeper view into the kingdom of resurrected love.

2.

OFFICE IN THE CHURCH

1. THE QUESTION AT ISSUE

THE chief stumbling block which non-Catholics come up against in the Church is authority, the impersonal institution. The paradox implied in the duty to follow Christ, the imitation of the inimitable, may—indeed must—be accepted: this dialectic of the impossible which is yet imposed as an obligation, of a gift that goes beyond all human capacity, in fact accords with the specifically Protestant sentiment. But what, we might well ask, can the most personal of all relationships and experiences, those of vocation and discipleship, have to do with an authority which can still function substantially despite personal sinfulness? Surely the whole logic of the Gospel teaching must make us regard it as a mere means of preserving social order within the Christian community? Above all, the whole course of development from the old to the new covenant seems to lead in quite a different direction. Even in the old covenant there was little about authority, and great stress laid on personal discipleship in faith and the people's obedience in faith as its history proceeded. In addition, such wide scope was allowed to free prophecy that it constantly checked and censured both the priesthood, hardened in its official ways, and the institutional kingship, and spared no one in recalling religion to its point of departure, namely, God's great decision for the people, comprising, as it did, the people's decision for God, their side of the nuptial relation.

And now that the old order ought to be infinitely surpassed through God's coming in the flesh, through the wholly unexpected way in which discipleship in faith has been made a concrete reality as given by one man to another, it is inconceivable that we should revert to a stage of religion outside of and prior to the biblical. Yet this is just what the Catholic Church does when she gives, as it were, an independent status to institutional organs and their functioning.

For the most part, the arguments in defense of the institution fail to meet the real objection or to allay disquiet. On the one hand, they merely refer the "structures" to Christ's positive ordinance, corroborated by an interpretation of relevant texts, and linked up with proofs drawn from history. On the other hand, they point to the logical necessity of the institutions from the religious aspect, their object being to safeguard the functioning of the sacramental system and ecclesiastical jurisdiction from dependence on the "worthiness" of the person exercising it. This is easily done by adducing the disastrous consequences brought in by the sects and heresies. But this second argument does no more than commend the acceptance of *minus malum,* or perhaps a *medium sine qua non,* which should be used with great care and delicacy as the pure means to an end, which is the personal following of Christ on the part of the believer. The first argument, based on the positive ordinance of the Founder of the Church, from which there can be no appeal, cannot easily satisfy human or even theological reason, or lead the *fides quaerens intellectum* to a tranquil contemplation of the doctrine. Must we, then, continue to endure a residue of unease about the institutional Church, as long as we are the *civitas Dei peregrinans,* and only afterwards, when the institutional part is no more, be able to look back and see its necessity and justification? Surely, this is one of the mysteries of the faith, all of which are solidary with the cross of Christ. It is one of the mysteries of the Church who, not only in her inmost being as the community of saints and the spotless bride of Christ, but also in her visibility to the world and her conspicuous imperfection, remains a pressing enigma. The answer to the difficulty, which concerns Catholics and non-Catholics alike, can be found only if personal discipleship and authority are seen as intimately connected from the very first, and inseparable both in fact and idea. And this connection must mean not only that the personal practice of the believer is protected and guaranteed externally by an impersonal authority (this may well be true, but it does not dispel all doubts), but also that the very concept of discipleship, which can only be apprehended dialectically, only *per excessum,* implies that of authority, and is inseparable from it.

The following study proposes to get back to that origin. It will, therefore, not be concerned with bringing out what is called a "unity of tension," such as is said to exist, for instance, between personal charisma and impersonal authority, in St. Paul's theology of the Church. There, the two are very closely linked so that, on a cursory view, authority could be seen simply as one charisma among others, and subsumed under this superior concept, though the subsequent independence of the authoritative office is seen as already in prospect, or even realized. The drawback here is that this view paves the way for the argument that the institutional side, from the human and sociological standpoint, is merely the inevitable residue left over when the tide of the first enthusiasm had ebbed, when the tremendous founder personalities such as Christ and Paul had left the scene to lesser men, and the charismatic succession—as in the Old Testament judges and prophets and (according to Max Weber) in many non-Christian religions—had ceased. Is this cessation, then, to be ascribed to a law of sociology and history governing the decay of enthusiasm? If so, the whole outcome is a betrayal of the Founder's intention, and a vindication of Protestant criticism of Catholicism. Or did it come about because the institutional factor is, of its nature, inseparable from the New Testament idea of discipleship? If so, and only then, the Catholic case is proved convincingly. But if it can be definitely established, important consequences follow for the common understanding of the Catholic Church. For if the two are really found to have been bound together in unity from the beginning, the Catholic Church

46

and the Catholic way of life can only be made credible and lived in view of this origin. Here, and here alone, is the real crux of all apologetics; and all the separate proofs derive their ultimate force from this unity forged by Christ and indissoluble.

This bond of unity between discipleship and authority once proven, it is capable of being understood in various—even contradictory—senses; and it is consequently here, at the very outset, that decisions must be taken which condition all that follows.

The first decision is whether the apostles' following of Christ as recorded in the Gospel was, of its very nature, directed to the office they were to be given; whether, that is, it was expressly a training for their authoritative position. Or, alternatively, whether it was a training for the Christian life in general and would only later, as if accidentally, issue in their consecration and official mission.

The second alternative is the one that any Christian free of preconceptions would spontaneously accept, seeing in Christ's relationship with his apostles a model for his own relationship with the Lord, and desirous of applying to himself piecemeal the Lord's instructions to his disciples. But that would make the institution of the office something more like a mere appendage to the general initiation into the Church and so pave the way to a positivism which reduces the spiritual office to a decision of Christ to be accepted without further explanation.

The first alternative is the one that commends itself naturally to the *fides quaerens intellectum* which spontaneously assumes an intimate connection between office and Christian living; but its acceptance would entail even more inacceptable consequences. For in this view the life of God among men, as described in the Gospel, would at its profoundest level be directed to the establishment of the clerical body—would, in fact, be a *"grand séminaire"* for the clergy on whom, after the ascension of the Founder, would devolve the task of handing on to the people the instruction imparted to them in virtue of the powers committed to them alone. Thus the spirituality of the Gospels would be preëminently a clerical one; and from this, two opposing

47

conclusions could be drawn. Either the spirituality of the laity must be derived from that of the clergy (somehow adapted and watered down in the process); or else lay spirituality cannot be formally contained in the clerical and must therefore be newly formed as something on its own according to the special state of life of the laity who occupy, in the order of the world, a position quite different from those who "have left all."

Both conclusions must be rejected as complete distortions and harmful in the extreme. Can there be a third way? Is it possible from one and the same history to extract both the universal and the particular, both what applies to all Christians and what applies solely to those in authority, without unwittingly falling into one extreme or the other?

The second option is closely bound up with the first; and the fact that it approximates it without being identical with it, throws light on the profound mystery of the Church that is already present in the first option, and rules out any hasty solution. The apostles had to leave behind all things in order to place their all in Christ, and it was into this void that the grace of their office was poured. But not everyone who leaves all things receives the exercise of authority; and not every layman literally leaves all. The distinction between the religious state and the secular cuts across that between the priestly state and the lay. All the theologians of patristic times and the Middle Ages saw, in the practice of the apostles, the foundation of the New Testament priesthood and of the discipleship of the individual Christian; and now we can either derive from it the obligations of the clergy, assimilating them to the rule of life of the apostles and the primitive Church (the regular clergy), or, alternatively (for instance, with Cardinal Mercier), direct the Orders to conform to the original order of Christ (the apostolic clergy) as their ideal and model. In both cases the laity are once again excluded, and we have the same dialectic as before. Either it is true, as an unbroken tradition from the Fathers to post-Reformation theology teaches, that the religious state in the Church today is what the whole Church was in the time of the apostles (in

48

Jerusalem, with its community of possessions); and then the state of the ordinary laity is a concession, something outside of the original perfection of the Gospel. Or else clergy and religious alike are restricted to representing a mere function within the total organism of the Church; but then it is difficult to see why the Gospel confines itself to explaining this special function, and the temptation arises to supplement this—historically conditioned?—onesidedness of the New Testament writings by an approach more suited to our time.

Here, too, it is enormously difficult to synthesize the various standpoints, even when we view the question from a distance; particularly when we remember that, as a matter of history, every genuine renewal of the ecclesiastical spirit has necessarily been effected by a return to the radical position of the first age, which was undoubtedly that of the "special" way of leaving all things. But the question now begins to take on a more acute form, for the issue concerns not only the lay state but the relationship, within the apostolic state, between spiritual office and spiritual life. If the spiritual office demands a spiritual mode of life as exemplified in the religious state, does it not follow that we must consider the ordinary form of life of the secular clergy as itself a concession and a compromise, compared with the strictness of the apostolic way of life?

There is yet a third option to be considered. It is true that the twelve chosen by the Lord form the new, spiritual Israel. They are to judge the twelve tribes; they constitute the twelve gates of the heavenly Jerusalem. But the significant factor is that they are not themselves tribes but individuals, and that the new people of God is built on the "foundation" of individuals who follow the unique individual Christ. It is only the individual who is called to follow Christ. Although the twelve form a *collegium,* they are individuals still, and not a collective, and their mission from the very beginning envisages each of them as being distinct from the others, each a missionary, on his own, to a particular country or district. At least this is the idea that follows from St. Matthew's account of the final sending forth of the apostles.

It is true that in reality things turned out a little differently (for most of the apostles, it was a matter of a little missionary work in the environs of Jerusalem), but was not this collective dwelling together already a departure from the original idea? And was it not actually the beginning, the foundation for the "impersonal" character of the office? It might be rejoined that a visible community on earth, such as Christ willed the Church to be, necessitates a properly constituted body as legislature and judicature, in which the individual plays a part only insofar as he holds any office. All this is true; but we must not be too hasty to equate the visibility of the community which is the Church with that of the natural community, and univocally to subsume both under the same general concept. Granted that the Church is a visible community, and further, that there is within the Church a purely official element and not only a personal charisma; can its character as community and as official body be determined and defined according to the laws of the natural community? Is it not rather the case that everything rests on the primary cell of personal discipleship, which is something quite different from the primary cell of the family; on *rebirth* which is essentially personal, as opposed to *birth* which is merely natural? In these days the question is posed in terms of an antithesis between a Church of the people and a missionary Church of individual missionaries; and although the manner of its resolution has far-reaching consequences, it may perhaps be reduced to a question of style in the conception of the Christian way of life. And even then, it very much affects all aspects of the Church's life.

2. THE PARADOX OF THE FOLLOWING

The whole course of relationships between Jesus and men starts from his command "Follow me" (Mk. 2, 14; Mt. 9, 9; Lk. 5, 27; Jn. 1, 43). This laconic injunction demands, moreover, immediate response, and it envisages the whole of life, and even more: existence in time and in eternity. It has the unconditional sense of the nearly literal equivalent "going along behind"; and only then has it the profounder meaning of a spiritual alignment behind him whose call is a command.

The response to his call is described as an equally immediate leaving all things and following him (Mt. 4, 20. 22; Mk. 1, 18; 10, 28; Lk. 5, 11; Jn. 1, 39). It is essentially a leap into the void where there is nothing but Jesus, —as we see in Peter's simple statement in Mark: "Behold, we have left all things and followed you." Here the question is not yet formulated which Matthew appends: "What, then, shall we have?" Here is a human question caught up within the answer inspired by the Lord, a question that cannot be suppressed nor is totally overshadowed by the fact of discipleship.

This step, or leap, is, for Jesus, the condition of their becoming disciples. We see this in the episode of the rich young man where, once again, the interpreting gloss in Matthew is originally lacking ("If you would be perfect . . ."), and it only says, "You lack one thing; go, sell what you have and give to the poor, and you will have treasure in heaven; and come, follow me" (Mk. 10, 21).

These three factors in conjunction constitute the gate to life with Christ. In the call, everything relates solely to the person calling. There is no set program about the way, or instruction to be followed, no ideal proposed, no law given to mark out the territory. There is no connection with anything known beforehand, no commendation of good will; no vows are taken. The follower is not praised for his courage or achievement; nor is he trained to make the leap, heartened by any inducement, warned about the gravity of the situation. The Lord does not first present himself, show his credentials in the manner of the head of a school, the master of an esoteric band of disciples. Everything consists in his mere call, which is his direct personal intervention, a claim on the one called. The call is absolute and, therefore, final; it is precisely the intervention of God's absolute sovereignty. Even when a miracle precedes (the draught of fish), or an appeal to an earthly teacher (John the Baptist), or to a prophecy of Scripture (as with Nathanael: see Jn. 1, 46, and

51

7, 41–42), all this fades into the background—or else it is so far surpassed as to become the direct contrary (the fishers become the fished; out of Nazareth, something good comes). Even the love that follows at a distance, when it encounters the one who turns towards it, can only ask, "Where do you live?", and from the moment of the "turning" (Jn. 1, 38), everything becomes a matter of the call and of going along with him.

The three disciples who recoiled from the starkness of "following" were dealt with uncompromisingly. The first, with his "I will follow you," assumed the initiative, the masculine role, and awaited the assent of the Lord. But no one can call himself, or let his enthusiasm be a substitute for the call. Jesus, far from unreservedly accepting him, showed him the void, which was his own inasmuch as he had nowhere to lay his head; but it appears as a void precisely because it is not filled by the call and so made tolerable. In fact, the void is all the deeper in that the man in question is a scribe, for whom the law and wisdom has always presented a content, *lucerna pedibus meis*. The second was a disciple, according to Matthew; Luke says that on the call "Follow me," he was at once accepted as a disciple. He asked first for permission to bury his father. The natural law, reënforced by the positive, obliged him. He felt himself not only in the right, but in duty bound, to frame a synthesis of the old and new covenants; first the old must be fulfilled, then he is free to go over to the new. But, as Jesus himself is the synthesis, it is for him, not the disciple, to frame it. "Let the dead bury their dead!" Everything apart from the God of the living (Mt. 22, 32) is dead, everything apart from Jesus, who is himself the life (Jn. 14, 6). He alone controls the law of nature and that of Scripture: "Of me Moses wrote," and therefore "If you believed Moses, you would believe me" (Jn. 5, 46). There can be no thought of violating a law through the following of Christ. The third said, "I will follow thee, Lord, but first let me take leave of those who are in my house." He was drawing up a program, dividing up the subject matter, mapping out stages of his development. If I can get so far, then I can take the risk. It reminds us of the scene in which Elijah casts the cloak of the prophet's calling on Elisha who was plowing with twelve yoke of oxen. "And he left the oxen, and ran after Elijah, and said, 'Let me kiss my father and my mother, and then I will follow you.' And he said to him, 'Go back again; for what have I done to you?' And he returned from following him, and took the yoke of oxen, and slew them" (1 Kgs. 19, 20–21), then followed Elijah, and became his disciple. The Lord said, "Whoso putteth his hand to the plow and looketh back is not fit for the kingdom of God." That is equivalent to "[he] cannot be my disciple" (Lk. 14, 27) and, more trenchantly, "[he] is not worthy of me" (Mt. 10, 37. 38).

The literal sense of "going along with" and (corresponding to the Jewish custom between rabbi and pupil) "coming after" (Mt. 16, 24) is so strong that it constitutes the indispensable basis for our understanding of the process, and this in three respects. In the first place, in that the pure, naked "going with" means, of itself, no more than local movement, does not include forward progress, instruction, consecration. The whole emphasis is on being with. This is more than a mere "coming to him," which, according to God's form of expression, is distinct from "discipleship" (Lk. 14, 26–27). It is, besides, more than a temporary "walking with," the characteristic of discipleship. In the New Testament, "following after" is so much of a real, active process that it is impossible to form from its verb form a general concept describing what is incumbent on all Christians, such as is the case with the noun "discipleship."

In the second place, the literal "walking with" and "being with" is the exclusive privilege of the twelve apostles, so much so that Paul, who was not then present, had the greatest difficulty in accrediting himself as an "appendage" of the apostolic college. For him there could not be a "following after" in the literal sense, since this was not possible at all in the time after the resurrection. In fact, there was not a "being with" as between one man and another, only a "being in"; and this, from now on, with the corresponding and complementary ideas of "turning

53

to the Lord," "calling by the Lord," "faith," expresses the new reality of Christian existence, until it takes on a new form, with the death of the body, though with a different meaning, that of "being with the Lord" (Phil. 1, 23). Here below, in the meantime, our "being with" Christ is changed into his being with us (see Mt. 28, 20).

Finally, in the third place, it was reserved to John, the last hagiographer of the new covenant, to undertake the synthesis of the synoptic literalness and the Pauline interpretation into something of universal and spiritual import. John was, from the beginning, present with Jesus. He was the first literally to accomplish the walking to Jesus and then with him (Jn. 1, 35–39, is undoubtedly autobiographical, and describes, prior to the calling of Peter, the characteristic quality of the beloved disciple). But this literal fact itself leads, in John's contemplation of it, to the ultimate spiritual step. Already, in the scene by the Jordan, each word has a spiritual overtone: the "hearing" of the Baptist's words, the "following" of Jesus, his "turning around," the mutual interrogation, the first appearance of the significant word "stay" ("Rabbi, where are you staying?"), especially the answer of Jesus, "Come and see," whose meaning is underlined by "They came and saw where he was staying; and they stayed with him"—here we have a summing-up of the whole Johannine theology. Thus John is the first to raise the idea of "following" from the literal and earthly plane to a spiritual one. He does so in connection with the twice repeated injunction of the risen Christ to Peter, "Follow me" (Jn. 21, 19. 22), meaning, as the context shows, to death and resurrection (not simply in "feeding the sheep" or to martyrdom or into the invisible world). Where Paul sees only a community of destiny between Christ and the Christian, John sees always the older, apostolic reality of the literal "following after and behind." This is something eternal and final, so that it is even the heavenly occupation of the elect: "It is these who follow the Lamb wherever he goes" (Rev. 14, 4). While preserving the apostolic prerogative, John has here opened up, for all who come afterwards, a breach through which they too (at a distance from the twelve) can enter on the "following." Already this had been done by the seventy-two, whose literal following of Christ is assured, but whose number itself (6 times 12) is symbolic, and therewith keeps the circle opened indefinitely.

Now the expression "going along with Christ" must have a very precise meaning and imply a very pressing necessity, not only for the person called, but for the One calling. To bring this out, let us first go beyond the bare literal aspect and face the real paradox of discipleship (or following). Its significance is, primarily, salvation and its attainment. God is salvation, which has now appeared in the form of man: to be in salvation means to be with this man. The identification of Jesus with salvation comes out in the great utterances he makes about himself in St. John, and also in those of the "Son of man" in the synoptics (Mk. 12, 6; 12, 37; 13, 26; 14, 21, 62). Whoever follows Christ unconditionally is "fit for the kingdom of God" (Lk. 9, 62). The rich young man seeks "eternal life," and Jesus responds to his searching with counsel to leave all and follow him (Mk. 10, 18. 21). In John, "following" is taken more spiritually as "not walking in darkness" and "finding the light of life," Christ himself being this light (Jn. 8, 12). It also means to gain participation in the messianic salvation, in the goods of salvation promised by the prophets, foreseen by Abraham, which "many prophets and righteous men longed to see ... and did not see" (Mt. 13, 17), but are now imparted, not to anyone at all, but to those who go with him and follow after him. Here we begin to glimpse the paradox: Why should salvation, which by its very nature, by the terms of its prophetic announcement, should be of universal application, be so incomprehensibly reserved to these elect? For it is that salvation "which thou hast prepared in the presence of all peoples, a light for the revelation to the Gentiles" (Lk. 2, 31–32). It is the visitation of the rising sun "to give light to those who sit in

55

darkness and in the shadow of death" (Lk. 1, 79), the preaching of salvation to all the poor, the blind, the bruised, and the captives (Lk. 4, 18). What is the explanation of this exclusiveness so insisted upon?

Certainly, we can understand that so great a good, a salvation so final and complete, is worth any sacrifice. It is perfectly in accord with reason, indeed with a commercial outlook, that one who has found the treasure in the field or the pearl of great price, should sell all in order to buy it (Mt. 13, 44–46). We can understand, in this light, that Jesus demands from those who desire to find him, the leaving of all the rest, hatred of all the rest, including the seeker himself (Lk. 14, 26)—as indeed is demanded by a right scale of values and a clear-cut decision—and, finally, the staking of one's own life, which is what the Church after the resurrection retrospectively included in the idea of "carrying the cross" (Mt. 10, 38; 16, 24; Mk. 8, 34; Lk. 9, 23; 14, 27). Before his own crucifixion, Jesus (who, in all his prophecies of the passion, had never once spoken of his cross) could not have demanded of his disciples a carrying of the cross as part of their following him. But he could demand that they stake their lives in their absolute decision to embrace the salvation offered by the Messiah. In the same way, the Lord addresses the demand to "hate" everything else and to "carry the cross" expressly to the "great multitude" (Lk. 14, 25–27), urging them to weigh up the entire consequences of his analogy of the "calculation of the cost" and the "king about to go to war" (Lk. 14, 28–33). All this he makes of general application. It concerns the arrangement incumbent on anyone if he is to participate in the goods of salvation at the end of time. In Christ this salvation is "at hand"; whoever draws near to him, who turns to him, attains it. If the twelve were no more than a visible representation, an example to make clear the meaning of this participation offered to all, there would be nothing paradoxical in their being called and requisitioned.

But this is not so, and it is just when we pursue the matter beyond this point of general application that the role of the

twelve seems so obscure and incomprehensible. For, since they
were chosen out especially, they were obviously more closely
united to the person, existence, and teaching of Christ with a
view to participating therein in a manner different from any
others. The question then arises: In what do they participate?
In Christ's teaching, through being more thoroughly instructed?
That is possible, but it cannot be the decisive point, since Christ
is not primarily a doctrine, but a life. In his life, then? That
too is possible, but cannot be the whole solution; for Jesus, and
he alone, was sent by the Father, to "give his life as a ransom
for many" (Mk. 10, 45); he alone is their "master," while
they are all brothers (Mt. 23, 8); finally, Jesus did not intend
for them to become themselves "teachers" later on: "Neither
be called masters, for you have one master, the Christ" (Mt. 23,
10). However marvelous their progress and sublime their functions, the original cleavage, the contrast that makes possible
all the rest, the fact that they are all "from below," and one
only is "from above," he who is "above all" (Jn. 3, 31–32; 8,
23), can *never* be bridged. Jesus is unique, he is the only-
begotten of the Father; he is what he does, and does what he is.

Undoubtedly, the Lord's public life had to do with the work
of teaching, and in what could he instruct the people and the
disciples if not in himself? He laid open to them his heart and
his feelings, for them to learn to understand him. He himself
is his doctrine. And since he is what he does, his disciples also
must do what he does and is, and, in so doing, gain some intimation of who he is (Jn. 7, 17; 8, 31–32); in so doing they
actuate, not themselves, but Christ in them. If this primary law
is forgotten through some kind of mysticism, however well-
intentioned or perfervid, Christianity is reduced to the level of
a merely human world religion based on one variety or other
of pantheism. It is against this that the Old Testament waged
war as against the age-old enemy: and the new covenant can
only mean the final victory of this conflict.

This unique relationship of master and disciple in the incarnation of God can, of course, be subsumed under human

categories, either sociological or ethical. Moreover, it is of the essence of the incarnation that this should be so, and that these categories apply, not only to the old covenant, but to the whole of human history in the natural order. In Greek religious philosophy there was a "following of God," a placing of oneself behind God, his leading, his providence, his will, as is so excellently expressed in the hymn of Cleanthus. What is small and peripheral orders itself to what is great and central. There is also the religious following of the wise man and teacher, through whom, in a covenant of discipleship, it was alone possible to attain, preserve, and transmit wisdom—consider Pythagoras, or Epicurus. Admittedly, the Old Testament idea of a covenant had its sociological basis in the covenants of the great nations and the nomadic tribes with their own special god to whom they pledged themselves and swore fidelity, and whom they "followed," literally in the case of the nomads, spiritually in the case of the higher cultures. And in the journey through the desert, Yahweh became, in reality, a God "going before" (Ex. 13, 21; 33, 16; Num. 14, 14; Deut. 1, 30. 33; 20, 4; 31, 6; and etc.), who jealously watched that they should "go after" him and not after strange gods (Deut. 6, 14 f.), not "to the right hand, or to the left," but straight "in all the way" (Deut. 5, 32–33). Yet, though this was an instance of the recognized fact of divine leadership, it went beyond the generality of such cases, being of a wholly unique character. Any parallels to it in religious history are far remote; they serve rather to obscure than to clarify its nature. That is why the old covenant speaks preferably of God "going before" rather than of the people "following." The latter term was chiefly employed negatively, not "going after strange gods," and, when positively, with an erotic overtone: Israel followed God in the desert as the Oriental bride followed her bridegroom (Jer. 2, 2). Generally, the injunction was simply to "walk in the way" of the Lord (Deut. 5, 33). Yahweh is no "wandering God," and the walking behind the ark of the covenant has itself no magical significance. It is always a matter of following the law of the covenant, spiritual self-commitment to God's disposition, to his wisdom. And the sapiential books know that man's relationship to wisdom is simply one of prayer for being constantly kept in his following and his status of sonship. At the same time, there was, indeed, a danger that the "wise man" of Israel should approximate too closely the wise men of Greece and Egypt, insofar as he was one who, through his dealings with wisdom, had received the intrinsic quality of "being wise." In the same period, too, the rabbis gathered round them their own groups of pupils, who followed them in the street a few paces away as a sign of reverence. But then Jesus came at the right moment to restore and bring out fully the proper and original idea of following at a distance, the idea of the covenant of Sinai and of the prophetic teachings.

For in the old covenant the pillar of fire and the clouds were only figurative; and, after Israel had entered the promised land, the main thing was a spiritual walking in the ways of God. But now the following of the incarnate Son was not just figurative, but rather the expression, becoming ever more exact, of a relationship with God which made quite impossible any equating of the divine wisdom that commands with man's own wisdom that obeys. And while the rabbis, as the prophets before them and now John the Baptist, had their groups of pupils, and the disciples of Jesus seemed, to all appearances, just one such group (Jn. 4, 2), yet the instructions they received from their master left them always in a state of surprise and disarray, since he did not impart "wisdom"; in fact, everything about him, words and conduct, indicated that he himself was wisdom. Outward and inward following, whose unity was only adumbrated in the old covenant, were in Jesus put on the same level. A paradox, then: the more one desires to be a "master," the more one must remain a pupil. The significance of this paradox is far more profound than in the old covenant, or than in the case of the natural relationship of a pupil (say, to his guru). It is not

59

just a matter of remaining in an attitude of prayer, of preserving contact with the master, but of the literal "apart from me you can do nothing fruitful" (Jn. 15, 5).

3. THE MORE INTENSE PARADOX OF IMITATION

The universal religious relationship as subpersonal could favor the conception that the center of the finite person can and must be taken and absorbed into the center of the Godhead. In the old covenant it would have been inconceivable that "walking in the ways of God," the realization of his commands in the individual life, could have led to Yahweh's becoming immanent in the believer or the latter's absorption into Yahweh. All was at the personal level, just as modern personalism derives from the idea of the actualization of the old covenant in the Jews (so Stern, Scheler, Buber, Gabriel Marcel). Christianity has gone beyond personalism as it has gone beyond the old covenant, to reach a higher plane proper to itself alone, one which, from the standpoint of natural religion as well as biblical personalism, is bound to seem wholly paradoxical, — bound, therefore, to be misunderstood. The paradox is so sharp that it is constantly liable, even in Christian theology, to take the direction either of a religious and mystical impersonalism or of a Jewish personalism. A Catholic theology that relies too much on an abstract metaphysics of being and grace, and also liberal Protestant theology, tend to impersonalism; orthodox Protestantism tends to personalism.

The crisis of the biblical idea of "following" is reached with the intrusion of the idea of "imitation" into the New Testament. It is more or less understandable that one should be able to follow some unique personality at a distance prescribed by respect and love. But that one can and must imitate what, in virtue of his uniqueness, is inimitable, this seems, from the Christian standpoint—for there is no other, historically—a flat contradiction, if one knows what one is talking about. Granted that we make *a priori* an absolute distinction between an external sphere of qualities and actions that are, in some way, imitable (these of necessity would be principally the human ones), and a sphere which is absolutely inimitable, because divine and divine-human. But even a cursory view of the New Testament is enough to show that such a distinction is never made, and that, on the contrary, Christ is inimitable to the same degree in which he is proposed to his followers for imitation. Terminologically, following and imitation are poles apart, and the difference is one that Protestant theology is prone to emphasize to the fullest extent; and even where the biblical text makes unavoidable a minimum of "imitation," it gets around this with the dialectic of *peccator* and *justus*. In fact, this theology makes a point of never allowing us to overlook the element of "following" in "imitation," even in the Christian and paradoxical sense of "following." One may well ask, therefore, whether a scrupulous care not to say a word too much in this regard is not preferable to speaking blatantly and unguardedly of the Christian as *alter Christus* and of "isochristism" (as the ideal of the Graeco-Christian mystics). Obedience to the specific Christian grace is the safeguard against both extremes, not by balancing the two, but by retaining the paradox that is not to be solved in the conceptual sphere, and elucidated only in the mystery of the Trinity, which enters, through Christ, even into the life and consciousness of man, and makes derisory his most daring flights of thought. What we may call "imitation" in the Christian sense is no other than the disciples' following as conceived and ordained by Christ himself, whose "leaving all things" and "going with" him was changed from a material to a spiritual act, and carried out in all seriousness. This took place in four stages.

1. The doctrine of Christ is Christ himself, and so for the Christian the content of Christian existence is nothing other than its form, namely, following. This is not merely the act of entering on a course of instruction (matriculation), but is

identical with it. Leaving all things means a spiritual renunciation of one's own views, mode of life, and purposes, and, on
a deeper level, of one's own freedom and reason, offering them
all to the Master, and, according to his disposition, either receiving them back or not, or having them replaced by his own
purposes and freedom and reason. In this, leaving all things
is the same thing as *faith*. The old covenant prepared the way
by raising the impersonal basic act of natural religion to the
plane of the personal. This act is the abdication of finite subjectivity in view of the infinite ground of all things. In Zen
Buddhism there is a similar mysterious exchange: the total renunciation of finite consciousness, knowledge, and power leads
to investiture with the infinite consciousness, knowledge, and
power. What is here a kind of technique, and so concealed
magic, is purified in the personal encounter between Yahweh
and the people, and assumes the form of self-commitment into
the hands of God to dispose of as he pleases. The religious
man does this, not in order to be immersed in the universal
reason, but that the personal design of God in his freedom
may be glorified in him. Hence the simile of nuptial and bridal
fidelity applied to Yahweh and Israel, which, despite the Oriental subordination of the woman to the man, is the product of
a genuine relationship between two persons.

Christian faith surpasses both forms. If we consider it in its
first, most primitive form, there is an unmistakable likeness
to the forms of the natural religions. In Mark, faith is the medium (of surrender) by which man *is able* (through surrender). Whoever can so give himself as Christ intended, indeed
as Christ himself did: in him can the supernatural take place.
Unbelief prevents miracles of healing (Mk. 6, 5). The belief,
however, of the haemorrhaetic woman causes a power to go
out from Jesus to heal her; her faith made her whole (5, 28. 34;
see 10, 52). Faith demands an act of spiritual courage to leave
all things and take the leap—hence the exhortation, "Do not
fear, only believe" (5, 36)—courage to bring the soul into
unity (Jas. 1, 5; Mt. 6, 22; Lk. 11, 34), and to discard double-

mindedness (Jas. 1, 8; 4, 8). Paucity of faith essentially leads to godlessness; but from "Take heart . . . have no fear" (Mk. 6, 50; 10, 50) to "Have faith in God" (11, 22) is but a step. The essential point is the reference to God, which means, for Christ, to the Father who sent him (Mk. 9, 37); the act of faith, mediated by Christ, has the Father for object. But what Christ taught he performed in superlative fashion. While those of little faith trembled in the storm, he slept in the boat; and, though his attitude may not be described as "faith," yet it is the model and prototype of faith. Afterwards, when he reproaches them and asks, "Have you no faith?", he means "faith in God," his own attitude, which he is educating the disciples in. There is also, in this connection, the case of the father of the possessed child, who said to Jesus, "If you can do anything, have pity on us and help us." Jesus, taking up the man's own words, replied, "If you can!" And he continued, "All things are possible to him who believes." The man replied, "I believe; help my unbelief!" Can the "believer" (who "can" do all) be referred to the man? Certainly not apart from Christ, who must assist the transition from double- to single-mindedness. Can the "believer" (who "can" do all) be referred to Christ? Certainly not apart from the man, for whom he is the prototype of oneness of faith and the power of faith. Only with the power of Christ, in it and through it, "can" the man elicit the faith necessary for the miracle to happen. It is the power of Christ that takes over in him, just as the Spirit of Christ will later take over in the disciples, so that they need take no thought beforehand of what they are to say (Mk. 13, 11).

Here we have a contrast with the Zen teacher, who prepares and trains the wise as to how one can let the infinite spirit work powerfully in the individual; a contrast, too, with the prophet, to whom it can be given, with his office, to impart to others God's Spirit (which he is not and which does not belong to him)—see Numbers 11, 25 f.; 2 Kings 2, 9–10. 15. St. John indicates what makes possible this higher condition in the Trinitarian formula, "For as the Father has life in himself, so he has granted the Son also to have life in himself" (Jn. 5, 26), so that he is neither indigent in his dependence nor unrelated to another in his power to dispose of his own being. His autonomy, as real as the Father's, has yet, as its inner form and prerequisite, his eternal sonship and love for the Father. This divine and divine-human form is the prototype of the Christian; he is exercised in it; moreover, as unique and inimitable, it is preëstablished both ontologically and ethically. For this reason, the relationship between the Christian and Christ is not simply a transposition, made possible by the incarnation, of the personal relationship between the people and Yahweh onto a human plane. For Christ exercises men in faith in the Father; faith in him, of its very nature, goes further ("He who believes in me, believes not in me"—Jn. 12, 44), and can never remain interpersonal; it is only possible as relating to the Trinity. And for the same reason the Christian act of faith is not totally comprehensible as a personal act, but, though it is that, the crucial element is that it is supra-personal and Trinitarian, which is what makes it possible.

The general structure is thus elucidated. The leap involved by "following," leaving all things (spiritually as a completely interior act), is, in its single-mindedness and courage, sustained from the very outset by the grace of Christ. This makes the double-minded participate in his divine and hypostatic oneness, and thus—again, purely in his grace—makes possible the following of him, and empowers the Christian not only to make the leap away, but to "come to him"; not only to follow, but to "imitate." This will be clearer in what follows.

2. There corresponds to the demand for total faith and the power imparted to make the leap, Christ's revelation of his own being in its fullness. Every one of his words, every act, points to the full meaning of his existence. It is impossible, therefore, to distinguish what is to be imitated, from the inimitable. In fact, it is precisely the inimitable things about him, the mes-

sianic miracle working, such as casting out devils and raising
the dead, that are enjoined upon the disciples. What is inimitable becomes imitable, for it is not so much the material act
which is put forward as the model, but rather the inmost unity
of the person performing it, his unity of sentiment, that is revealed. It is never anything material that is offered for imitation, not even in the case of the washing of the feet, whose
copying is expressly demanded, but always the spiritual core
shown forth in the particular expression. One must always look
to the heart. For this reason, the acts of Jesus can be not only
unlikely but astonishing, and both together, for it is precisely
the lowliness of the Lord in becoming a servant that is the
astonishing thing, the more one comes to understand it. The
opening of his heart in Matthew 11, 25–30 (Lk. 10, 21–22)
begins with his praise of the Father, who has hidden it from
the wise, meaning both the pagan wise, who aimed at finding
the infinite only through their own finitude, and the Jewish
wise, who had falsely usurped the divine wisdom, without possessing the simplicity of faith. The "simple," the "little ones,"
however, gain a participation through grace, not actually in the
Son nor the Father, but in the sphere of the mutual relationship of Father and Son, in which the Spirit moves. This is a
sphere completely unapproachable by those who stand outside,
but made accessible by the gracious good pleasure of the Son.
It is the sphere to which the simplicity of the child is alone
commensurable, and which is envisaged by the passages concerning children (Mk. 9, 36–37; 10, 13–16; see 24). The
heart that is now revealed and that reveals him is gentle and
humble, so that it is the expression of the Spirit and gives it
place for its dwelling. It is not "following" that the Lord demands, but "coming to him," to be lightened from the "yoke"
of the law, "which neither we nor our fathers were able to bear"
(Acts 15, 10), and by him will be changed and become "sweet
and light," in that the heart itself (which makes known the
heart of God) becomes the "law" of the "little ones." This
heart will itself take up the "yoke" of the cross, of the scorn

and mockery of all men, and the extreme of hatred. Here, however, it demands, not the following of the cross as an ascetic practice, but only "coming to him," submission to God's own law of the heart. But, as we have seen, the demand for this submission makes submission impossible.

On that account, the words of Jesus to men are shrouded in a strange obscurity. Insofar as they convey a demand to those in grace, the elect, they give access to him and understanding; otherwise, they bring about non-understanding and scandal, exclusion. The parables are theological forms of speech, since they reveal enough to make faith possible, and conceal enough to make unbelief possible. And it is just this "hearing and understanding" or "hearing and not understanding" that forms the content of the first great parable, that of the sower, who is the Son of man himself (Mt. 13, 37). Christ, when he expounds the kingdom of God in parables, necessarily expounds himself, not, however, as a "doctrine," but as the reality to which man can only say yes or no.

In this consists its difference from the invitation of Wisdom in the words which sum up the old covenant: "Draw near to me, ye unlearned: and gather yourselves together into the house of discipline. . . . And submit your neck to the yoke: and let your neck receive discipline. For she is near at hand to be found. Behold with your eyes how I have labored a little and have found much rest to myself" (Ecclus. 51, 31. 34–35). This wisdom at rest in itself after a little labor is in contrast with the open heart of God which receives all the humbled in its own humiliation that they may find rest, and can only do so by giving them to share this yoke of humiliation. In consequence, the yoke of the new law leads directly on to the yoke of the cross which the Christian, in his following, has to take on himself. If we want to set out all the implications of "carrying the cross" according to the words of Jesus, we notice that the expression could not have been used before Peter's confession (Mt. 16, 16; Mk. 8, 29; Lk. 9, 20; Jn. 6, 68–69)—in Matthew 10, 38, therefore, it is used in anticipation. In it we have the inmost depths of Christ's heart revealed to the fullness of faith of the twelve (Mt. 16, 21), and in the heart of Christ the exposition of the Trinitarian decree from eternity (Jn. 1, 18; 3, 16). Once again, it is not the exterior act but the interior sentiment that, as God's attitude and settled disposition, is transfused unreservedly into the faith of the Church. The follower and imitator of Christ is initiated into this attitude of God, and not into his unique and inimitable act of redemption, in such a way that he is primarily given the charge, not to perform something, but to let the disposition and the consequent act of God come to pass in himself; or rather, to see himself as admitted to this attitude and act of God as his true sphere, from which follows, in the absolute logic of revelation, the "go thou and do in like manner." And since God's unique resolve to redeem in forgiveness was taken in eternity, the attitude of the Christian also has an element of eternity, reaching beyond all temporal standards ("seventy times seven"—Mt. 18, 22), and immune to all objections based on personal reciprocity (Mt. 5, 20 f.). It is therefore something outside all human probability, impressive, striking, and demonstrative (Jn. 13, 35).

This is the context in which to view the few texts in the Gospel which speak of "imitation" rather than of "following." In Matthew 11, 29, we have "learn from me," learn, that is, the meekness and humility which reflect, for men, the heart of God, and which itself should be reflected in the disposition and actions of man, as the parable of the unmerciful servant shows. The two other passages also directly envisage the interior disposition. The first (Mt. 20, 26–28) is Christ's instruction occasioned by the petition of the mother of the sons of Zebedee: ". . . whoever would be great among you must be your servant, and whoever would be the first among you must be your slave; even as the Son of man came not to be served but to serve, and to give his life as a ransom for many." Here we have the first teaching; the example follows as a kind of appendage, an illustration, a confirmation by the most extreme instance. This doctrine, so opposite to all exercise of power in the world (v. 25), is, in order to be shown as practicable, hidden in the special sphere of the Lord. For the act of the Son of man which is adduced in elucidation—his act, which sums up in itself all that is peculiarly his—is precisely what is inimitable and unique. Here we are not taken so far as we are later by St. John, when he demands that because "he laid down his life for us ... we ought to lay down our lives for the brethren" (1 Jn. 3, 16). Only by way of parenthesis had the Gospel previously said the same: "This is my commandment, that you love one another as I have loved you. Greater love has no man than this, that a man lay down his life for his friends" (Jn. 15, 12–13). Matthew emphasizes the disparity: only the Lord can give his life as a redemption; it is for the disciples to make theirs the disposition to be servants and to strive for the lowest place (see Lk. 14, 7–11). Following the Lord to his own cross can be promised by the Lord only after his resurrection as the most excellent of graces (Jn. 21, 18), and as such its full implications were worked out by St. Paul.

The doctrine, also, on the occasion of the washing of the feet (Jn. 13, 13–17), which contains the word "example," is still a doctrine of love humbling and abasing itself; though the element of imitation, in fact the strict command of imitation, only comes in the second place, whereas the first explanation, made in the course of the action, gives it a sacramental character and therefore one inimitable by the disciples. What Jesus alone can do, —to give, through the washing, community with himself, that is, to take man's sins on himself—, that Peter cannot. But the disposition in which the Lord does what cannot be imitated, Peter can and must imitate through the outward example and inward grace of the Lord. This distinction seems the solution, but is it really? Is it possible, in the case of the Lord himself, to distinguish disposition and action? Is not the disposition—in the very act of washing the feet—the love that goes "to the end" (Jn. 13, 1), and so to the cross? And how should a sinner "imitate" this disposition of the utmost purity, indeed proper to the Godhead, unless the miracle of sacramental washing precedes, carrying over all the feeble and fragile work of the sinner into the very sphere of Christ with all its efficacy at once human and divine?

3. The point at which following can become imitation, that of "having the same mind as Christ Jesus" (Phil. 2, 5), is the heart and the total of all Christian ethics, as summarized by Matthew in the Sermon on the Mount. It runs through all the individual commandments, not to develop them in a material sense, but to bring them under the permanent Christian form, which is nothing less than Christ's own personal way of thinking. It is always pointing the way from promise to fulfillment, while emphasizing how close the promise is to its fulfillment (the beatitudes), and yet how clearly fulfillment goes far beyond promise. The ethics of Christ is an exposition of his personal way of thinking, only to be understood in the light of his own personality. It is not framed in view of man and his possibilities, but in view of Christ and what is possible to God. Thus it extends to the renunciation of one's rights, and of power, and even of one's honor, which the natural law enjoins every man to preserve. It even goes so far as to eliminate the distinction between friend and enemy, and not merely by way of counsel, but of command; not as a remote ideal, but as a condition for entering the kingdom of heaven (Mt. 5, 20), for obtaining the Father's forgiveness of sin (6, 14–15) and for avoiding God's judgment (7, 1). Human laws expressing the relationship between reality and appearances are subjected to a remorseless criticism; not because social religion is to be changed into something individual, but because both, the social and the individual aspects, are assessed according to the attitude of the incarnate God. Thus "good works" done in public, prayer in public, fasting in the public view, give way to what the Father sees in secret. The command not to be solicitous means that the criterion is not the nature of the external work but God's judg-

ment, showing that the whole ethic is constructed in view of God and the perfection of the "Father in heaven." It is the ethic of "But I say to you," justifying such a displacement of values, since he vindicates the most ignominious of humiliations and sufferings on the part of his followers: "Blessed are you when men revile you and persecute you and utter all kinds of evil against you falsely on my account. Rejoice and be glad" (5, 11–12). From now on, what is to be made visible is the glory of the cross. That is the city set on a mountain, the light in the candlestick, the good work that must shine before men, so that they may see it and praise the Father.

The problem raised by this ethic seems insoluble, for it is undoubtedly an ethic for men. Each commandment taken by itself seems a possibility, something within human fulfillment, so much so that the Sermon on the Mount has been seen as a summing up of the humanistic attitude. Yet, taken as a whole, it is certainly beyond human capability, utopian or eschatological. It is something that takes no account of real human relationships in all their complexity, something wholly out of this world and above it, and therefore undermining the foundations of human society. If anyone does not feel this, he has never experienced a single breath of the scorching, piercing air of the Gospel. Protestant attempts at a solution have this much in their favor, that they bear witness to an experience of the shock of these words. Such an attempt is the idealistic Kantian solution of the liberals, who see Christ's demands as a kind of ideal scale of values, an eternal standard by which reality is to be measured. Another is the eschatological solution of the radical followers of Schweitzer, for whom the Sermon on the Mount can only be seen as a (utopian) interim ethic valid till the judgment shortly to come to pass. Then there is the dialectical solution of the Barthians and the later Lutherans, for whom the whole program is actually carried out only by Christ; in him alone *peccatores* are *justi,* and Christians bear witness by their attempt to bring this program into the light. All three realize the vast, humanly unbridgeable gulf between man's real condition and the reality here demonstrated. There can never be any question of transition, approximation, advance from one to the other, in the sense of from below to above. In consequence, it can only be a matter of a lofty guiding ideal or of an eschatological miracle, with which the sinner, as such, has nothing to do.

None of these approaches to a theological ethic is adequate to compass the whole situation as given; but they do all face the difficulty that arises from the disparity between the human and divine standpoints. The same cannot be said of the pure religious and social ethic which presents the Sermon on the Mount as simply a program to be realized in the sphere of the inner sentiments as Christian and human; and yet this ethic, in contrast with the other three, takes account of one side of the matter as given, namely, the sober duty of man to fulfill the program. It must, indeed, be fulfilled, but this is not humanly possible. It is possible, though, in Christ, quite apart from assuming any dialectical or idealistic gulf between the realities of earth and heaven. It is, in fact, possible in the contact between the faith that "follows" and the divine heart opening itself through grace, in the contact made by the believer in leaving all things, so as, without reflection on himself (for he must abandon and "hate" himself), to approach the Lord and, with the Lord, his Father and his human brethren. His part is to make an act of obedience in faith, and his attitude must be one of surrender to the Lord which allows himself to be informed by him. In this respect, the Christian life is, in the strictest sense, above and beyond all psychology.

The point we have now reached is the source of the Christian mission, which, however, in its theological structure, has already reached the stage at which authority in the Church, in the strict sense, comes into being. Where the paradox of "following" results for Protestantism in a dialectic is just where, for Catholics, it results in mission and office. For the Catholic these are not factors that make it possible for man, of himself, to conjure away the disparity involved in the idea of "following"; they are what God himself takes into his own hands to end the disparity. "With men this is impossible, but with God all things are possible" (Mt. 19, 26). For God as Creator is a God of form and of the beautiful; for his greatest works he makes use even of sin and its consequences, and of the cross, too, which will not "be emptied of its power" (1 Cor. 1, 17). The act of surrender in faith under the impulse of grace is therefore answered by God with investiture with "the form of Christ" which will be formed in the Christian (Gal. 4, 19) so that he, in turn, may become a "form" for others (1 Thess. 1, 7). This form, as common to all Christians, is the soil from which springs authority in the Church, the "pattern for the flock" (1 Pet. 5, 3) which is a form specially established by Christ. It is not to be conceived democratically as derived from the first, but presupposes it, and thereby is understandable as a universal Christian element. The words "form" or "pattern" are makeshifts which cannot do justice to all the chief elements, notably the vitality and personality of the new life in Christ established by God, which Paul compares with "putting on" a garment, Christ himself (Rom. 13, 14; Gal. 3, 27), or dynamically, putting on "the new nature, which is being renewed in knowledge, after the image of its creator" (Col. 3, 10). Yet this image (which, to be properly understood, demands a full treatment of the ancient usage of clothing and assimilating, of walking along with and transforming, to mean the same thing, is, for us, something external, whereas "form" supposes an inner principle imposing a pattern, and this Paul is equally fond of using.

This form of Christ has its source in the, so to speak, material, feminine principle of the surrender of faith, "leaving all things," and in the formal, male principle of grace giving itself and imprinting itself on the believer, in whom it is a participation, in Jesus Christ, in the life of the Trinity. This life of grace, therefore, even insofar as it is "form," is by no means "impersonal." We must not misunderstand the statement, theologically unimpeachable, that God's natural works

72

OFFICE IN THE CHURCH

and supernatural graces *ad extra* are *communia*. It is, rather, "suprapersonal," in the sense of a participation in the vitality of the interchange of life between the three Persons. The Christian life, lived as it should be, is evidence and confirmation, though in a mysterious fashion and inexpressible in words, of this suprapersonal quality of life, for true holiness is always a psychological enigma.

The condition for its attainment is the right relationship between man and grace. The more pliable, abandoned, and free from his self-form the believer is, the better can the divine image and the form of Christ be impressed on him. *Ecce ancilla Domini.* Consequently, the less a man himself reaches out to a form, clings to one, and the more freely in "leaving all things" he holds himself ready for the reception of the form of God; and the less he reflects on his own creaturely being and fancies that he knows in advance who he is, the better the process of his being "put on" succeeds (2 Cor. 5, 2); and the more unhindered does Christ live in him as in one of his members, the Spirit live in him as in his temple (Gal. 2, 20; 1 Cor. 6, 15. 19). The faith that "leaves all" is, however, not one's own achievement. It is preceded by redemption through the blood of Christ, God's taking possession of man, the fact that "you are not your own" (1 Cor. 6, 19) and that, therefore, "those who live might live no longer for themselves but for him who for their sake died and was raised" (2 Cor. 5, 15). The believer is thus humbled by his faith (and through seeing what has been done for him), and his humiliation is the condition for his elevation by God (Mt. 23, 12; Lk. 14, 11; 18, 14). And the more the form freely given is imprinted on and consciously present to the individual and to the community, the greater must be the bearer's sense of humility, the more profound his abasement. This applies, above all, to the ministry in the Church; and equally to the mission demanding a special holiness. The form of the Christian as it develops never has the effect of eliminating the double paradox of "following" and "imitation"; in fact, it brings it our more sharply. The more

73

the servant, sent out and commissioned, represents the Lord—
not only externally by a function to be discharged, but internally by his life and person—the more profoundly does he see
himself in contradistinction to the Lord. As long as he is really
the Lord's servant, nothing can be further from his mind than
to equate himself, in any point whatever, with the Lord. Just
because he sets this distance between himself and the Lord, the
form of Christ and of God is infused into him. We may even
say that inasmuch as the servant more deeply feels himself to
be, on a quite other plane, different from the Lord, the more
like him he becomes, like him who took on the *forma servi,*
and was found "in habit like to a man," obedient even unto the
cross, so that he might come to know the extreme disparity
between the sinner and the Father, and, as God's Son, to sur-
mount it.

4. Now we must look closely at the investiture with the form
of Christ as shown in the Gospel, not as an isolated act, but in
its connection with the manifestation of Jesus himself. Once
again, it is Mark who takes us closest to the source. The beginning and end of his Gospel are governed by the idea of the
exousia, the fullness of power. Its manifestation is the main
point of the various callings recorded in the beginning.

There is first the exousia over the world of spirits. This is
preceded by the temptation by the devil and the ministration
of the angels in the desert, and followed by the calling of the
first four disciples, who leave all things. Then follows the first
showing of the exousia in the synagogue at Capharnaum, the
first outbreak of astonishment, the first encounters with unclean spirits (1, 23. 26. 27. 32. 34. 39). In 2, 10 f., the casting
out of the devil is both forgiveness of sins and a manifestation
of the exousia. Then there is the calling of the tax-collectors
and the feast with publicans and sinners, and the "I came not
to call the righteous, but sinners" (2, 17).

There is, secondly, the exousia over the law: that of fasting, which he declares inappropriate while the bridegroom is present; that of the sabbath, of which the Son of man is the Lord, as is evidenced both by the disciples plucking the ears of corn and by the healing of the man with the withered hand. The Pharisees are beside themselves with indignation, and already resolve upon his death.

And there is, in the third place, the imparting of his own unprecedented exousia to the disciples, recorded in the same sentence, practically, as their calling: "And he ... called to him those whom he desired; and they came to him. And he appointed twelve, to be with him, and to be sent out to preach and have authority [exousia] to cast out demons" (3, 13–15). This he repeats at the actual sending: "And he called to him the twelve, and began to send them out two by two, and gave them authority over the unclean spirits. . . . So they went out and preached that men should repent. And they cast out many demons, and anointed with oil many that were sick and healed them" (6, 7. 12–13). It was because of this that he was alleged to be possessed, and so gave his instruction about the unclean spirit and the Holy Spirit. The theme of his encounter with spirits is continued (5, 1–18; 6, 7. 12; 7, 25–29).

Finally, the question of exousia is again the central one: "By what authority [exousia] are you doing these things?" (11, 28); but the question is countered with another, and remains unanswered. The solution is given in the growing revelation of his sonship, manifested more and more as something sublime and unique (12, 6; 12, 37; 13, 26. 32; 14, 62; 15, 2; 15, 39). The final scene establishes once again and forever the exousia of those he sends forth (16, 17–18).

We see, then, a unique personality who, wherever he goes, arouses consternation and bafflement, working miracles while remaining in his state of solitude, somewhat like a meteor impinging on the world, proclaiming his power from above over the world of spirits, and asking from men no more than the courage to believe. And the most striking thing about it all is the suddenness with which his exousia is imparted to twelve men without education or preparation, with no period of transition; and then, so endowed, they are sent forth.

In the account in St. Matthew, the investiture with this power is no less sudden. There is, indeed, a distinction made between the passages where Christ speaks of the kingdom of God (the Sermon on the Mount, vv. 5–7) and that in which he sends out the twelve (v. 10). In the former, he speaks of the way of life in general; in the latter, of the conduct to be observed in the discharge of the ministry; on the one hand, of life in the world as a Christian among other men; on the other, of opposition to the world to which the apostle comes with his commission, from which he must guard himself, at whose hatred he is not to be surprised. The discourse on the kingdom is indeed delivered in the presence of a great multitude, but it is the disciples who come to him and whom he instructs (5, 2). The final beatitude of those who are persecuted "for my sake" and have evil spoken of them, is reinforced by allusion to "the prophets who were before you," obviously before the disciples. They are the salt of the earth, the city on a hill, the light on the candlestick; and, since the subject is not changed, it is to be assumed that all that follows is addressed to them, in the presence of the listening crowd. The Head of the Church is teaching the entire Church, consisting of clergy and people. There is no secret doctrine for the disciples; every word that concerns them in particular also applies to the whole Church in general, and whatever applies to the people applies in a special manner to the disciples.

Even the parables which he afterwards explains to his disciples apart, he first utters to the "great multitudes" (13, 1–2. 36). And so Peter, on the occasion of the parable of the watchful servant (Lk. 12, 35–40), can express the doubt: "Lord, are you telling this parable for us or for all?" The Lord answers by bringing out the nature of the Church's ministry, that of the faithful and prudent steward set over the household to give it food in season, to whom the Lord has entrusted the administration of all his goods. Since he knows his Lord's will, he will be held to a much stricter account than one who does not know it (12, 42–48). Likewise, the disciples are constantly admonished not to be, like the people, "without understanding" (Mt. 15, 16; 16, 9; Mk. 7, 18), for to them "it has been given to know the secrets of the kingdom of heaven," but not to the rest (Mt. 13, 11). It is, then, of slight importance that, in Luke, some of the Sermon on the Mount is preached to the "multitudes" (Lk. 11, 29 f.), some to his disciples in the presence of so great multitudes "that they trod upon one another" (Lk. 12, 1), and some only to his disciples as the "little flock" (Lk. 12, 22. 32). More significant is the fact that the doctrine of carrying the cross in the following of Christ and of the necessity of hating everything occurs, in Matthew, in the discourse to the twelve as they were sent on their mission (10, 37–38), but in Luke is addressed to the "great multitudes" (14, 25–27), and carrying the cross is designated as a "daily" necessity. Even the statement, "whoever of you does not renounce all that he has cannot be my disciple" (14, 33), is addressed to the whole people. This cannot be explained by a subsequent "ethicalization" of Christ's original and literal demand. Luke's is by no means a watered-down Gospel. The words of his Gospel, in fact, have a twofold meaning, just as they do in Matthew. In a narrower sense they are for a more restricted circle, and in a more general sense (though in no less a grave and literal way) they are for a wider circle. The distinction between the two circles is a somewhat fluid one, inasmuch as the mission discourse, taking up as it does apostleship, in Mark and Matthew is addressed to the twelve, but in Luke to the seventy-two (10, 1), who are expressly commissioned. But can we therefore say that the seventy-two are necessarily also invested with the ministry? Their being sent out "as lambs among wolves," without purse, scrip, or shoes, to announce the kingdom, heal the sick, and thus to be worthy of the reward, can also be applied in an unforced way to the laity, —say, to those Roman soldiers who, as they moved with the army from place to place, spread the kingdom of God everywhere. Why should not the closing words be applicable even to the seventy-two: "He who hears you hears me" (10, 16), since, according to the account they gave to the Lord of their mission, the spirits also were subject to them?

We may, indeed, try to establish a sharp distinction between those who follow in the literal sense—that is, all men or women who accompany the Lord in his journeys (Lk. 9, 1–3) —and those who do not or who are, in fact, prevented by the Lord, like the possessed Gerasene (Mk. 5, 18–20; Lk. 8, 38–39), who is subsequently given an "apostolate" in the midst of the world. But such a distinction is not altogether clear. The prohibition is made, in this case, more in view of the man's previous life than in order to establish an actual "lay apostolate." In any case, such a slender thread cannot be made to support a theological proposition. And then it is reasonable to consider the friends of Jesus in Bethany, who, though outwardly "lay people in the world," certainly belong inwardly to those who have "left all things," and, in their own fashion (Mt. 26, 10–13), fulfill a universal function in the Church. The same may be said of Mary Magdalen, with her function in the Church as representative of sinners redeemed, an office performed in the public life of Jesus, both beneath the cross and at Easter.

This is the general setting in which we should consider the various utterances of the Lord gathered together in Matthew 10 as his discourse to those he was sending out. There is no part of it that does not concern every Christian, but none also which does not receive special force and character from the circumstance of the sending of the twelve. Some parts were spoken to them in particular, and may, *per extensionem* or in special circumstances, be of application to all. Others primarily concern every Christian, and those in authority must simply pay special attention to them. These are such passages as: "A disciple is not above his teacher, nor a servant above his master; it is enough for the disciple to be like his teacher, and the servant like his master. If they have called the master of the house Beelzebul, how much more will they malign those of his household?" (Mt. 10, 24–25). In the end, the Christian who is sent is not given any privileged reception on the part of the world, whether he is one of those formally "sent" or one of the "prophets" or one of the "just," or simply "one of these little ones" (10, 40–42). The structure of existence, the "Christian form," is the same for all four.

Yet it would be a grave error to conclude from this that, in the new covenant, there is no more than a "universal priesthood," or that authority here is nothing but a universal charismatic quality in the Church more strongly imprinted on certain individuals. The twelve, chosen out by name from the very beginning and designated apostles in a specific sense, are they who were present from the outset and remained when most of the others left (Jn. 6, 66), who "continued with me in my trials" (Lk. 22, 28), who pronounced the decisive words of the confession and received the keys (Mt. 16, 18; 18, 18), were given the function and authority to celebrate the Eucharist and to bind and loose sins (Lk. 22, 19; Jn. 20, 23). It was to them as a college that the risen Christ appeared, to them he finally opened the meaning of the Scriptures (Lk. 24, 45), to them he imparted the final commission and the great apostolic promise (Mt. 28, 16–20). Office and power hold fast together, and are never impugned in the period covered by the Acts of the Apostles; St. Paul's whole theology of the apostolate presupposes their recognition. But this does not mean that the form of life of those in authority is essentially different from that of the others. It is, in fact, the same, and the Gospels confirm this in making no hard and fast distinction between them, without thereby prejudicing the universal transposition from the "flesh" to the "spirit," from an earthly and literal understanding to a spiritual and free interpretation. For the Son, in his mortal life, must speak and act within the world of time and space as one subject to death, but his words are "spirit and life" (Jn. 6, 63), and "shall not pass away" (Mt. 13, 31), because the Spirit hears and explains them (Jn. 16, 13), and makes them co-extensive with all time. In the same way, Jesus expressed in geographical terms his sending the disciples out into the world (Mt. 10, 5–6; Lk. 24, 47; Acts 1, 8), and the Spirit raises it to a higher potentiality in which Jerusalem, the geographical center and point of departure, is superseded, and the mission goes out everywhere from every place. Now everywhere is a "holy land" and everywhere is "strange" (1 Pet. 2, 11), and from out the mortal word comes forth the immortal meaning.

4. FORM AND IMITATION

The words *"âme"* and *"ôme"* mean "measure." To "amen" a vessel means to take its measure, its dimensions. And *"ahmen,"* *"nachahmen"* (to imitate) means to take the measure of a thing or person, so as to know it and in certain circumstances use it in the formation of new structures.

Christ had of necessity put himself forward as an example to his "pupils" and followers, even if this word is used only in John, and then only once (13, 15). The word and the idea remain in the background, because imitation involves the interplay of two meanings: imitation of what is absolutely inimitable, of one who is unique of his kind; and imitation of those who fail even in the presence of Christ, because in him on the cross sin is brought to the light of day. Never in the Gospel is the following, the imitation, of the Lord described as something to be achieved by degrees. The disciples are, to a great extent, stage figures, activated by the words of the Lord, by whose failures the Master demonstrates his own wisdom and infallibility, and over whom, quite unexpectedly, almost like a costume, the "armor" (Eph. 6, 11) of an apostle and messenger of Christ is suddenly thrown, along with all the powers appertaining to it: they are given a role with which they have to identify themselves. One may perhaps speak, on the plane of psychology, of a certain gradual "growing into" this role, but the decisive factor in their training is the cross and the absolute failure of Judas, Peter, and the rest who fled (even John slept and left the Lord alone). For what happened here was no fiction, no mere exercise in humiliation, but a real, fruitful humiliation which alone brought to successful conclusion the attempts to "leave all," and so made them capable of receiving authority.

The threefold denial is given an almost liturgical form in the Gospels, so that it is an essential part not only of the passion, but also of the ceremony by which the ministry is instituted. The threefold denial recalls the threefold, Trinitarian question, "Do you love me?" (Jn. 21, 17), and has the same liturgical and symbolic overtones as the upside-down crucifixion of Peter foretold immediately afterwards (21, 18–19). This fits in with the concluding passage, which disposes, with divine irony, of Peter's question in his official capacity about John's remaining (that of the Johannine Church within or without the Petrine): "What is that to you?" (21, 22–23). This brings out clearly the limits within which the holder of office in the Church is representative of Christ, and also, for the last time, the appropriate treatment of the ministry by the Head, one of honor combined with an ever renewed and intensified humbling. All of Peter's qualities as they become manifest—his well-meaning impulsiveness, his evasiveness at the prospect of the cross, his striking out from secret fear, the bravura of his faith which makes him lose his head when he comes to reflect—all these are used for humiliation, because "the greatest among you" must become as "the youngest, and the leader as the one who serves" (Lk. 22, 26). Peter is, with those like him, firmly grounded in the paradox of the ceremony of institution, and never forgets it. It is only thus, as stamped therewith, branded, that he can become an example to his flock (1 Pet. 5, 3). His denial is no chance occurrence, for nothing in the passion happens by chance. It is necessary as an essential element in the instilling of the "form" as foreordained for the way of life of those in the ministry. Once again: the "form" is not the ministry itself. It is the unity made up of the man as he is ("a failure") and the commission given by divine grace from above. This unity gives its determinate structure to the Christian life in general and to that of the ministry in particular, its authenticity for those endowed with supernatural perception, its wholeness unimpaired by all the criticisms of the world.

This form is always represented when the disciples, in the Acts, give testimony before Jews and Gentiles, before the Sanhedrin and the Roman officials. It is especially what St. Paul means when it appears in his writings as a distinct reality which has to be recognized and can be proposed to the community for imitation: "Brethern, join in imitating me, and mark those who so live as you have an example in us" (Phil. 3, 17). *"Typos"* is actually something hammered out, stamped out, an outline to guide, which withstands every kind of verification, and on which psychology, Christian or otherwise, breaks its teeth in vain. But here everything is enigmatic, and becomes more so the more it is analyzed and its individual characteristics and motivational forces distinguished. What St. Paul calls form is, however, indivisible, and the only motivational force in human events, even though it is rightly perceptible only with the eyes of faith.

This image impressed has no independent status, aesthetically or ethically. In other words, however perfectly it is realized in the person of the apostle, the person himself is quite secondary, in fact nugatory, for he does not make his own imprint or present himself, but is purely the material for the form and the power of God to make itself present. The *typos* can be, in a way, static, full, and perfect—and so really be put forward as an exemplar for imitation—while the person bearing it is still long engaged in struggle and imperfection. Hence the paradox of the Letter to the Philippians, which enjoins imitation of the supreme exemplar, Christ, with his sentiments of love and suffering (2, 5–11), and this "without grumbling or questioning" so as to become "blameless and innocent, children of God." And yet, this salvation is to be worked out "with fear and trembling," conscious, therefore, of one's own failings, and fearful of losing it. It is a question of realizing a perfect form in the extreme imperfection of personal effort, the two opposing extremes being united by the pure grace of God, "at work in you, both to will [personal, imperfect] and to work [achievement]" (2, 12–13). What is demanded of the faithful is once more demonstrated beforehand in the apostle, the one who has "left all" (3, 8), who, for that reason, is free and suitable for the office of being *typos*. For the image he offers and proposes has a real power of imprinting itself (3, 17), so much so that he enjoins them to look not only on this imprint, but on those already stamped with it, to walk according to them; nor does he hesitate to call them "perfect" (3, 15). Yet this static image only comes to be in that Paul is convinced that he has not yet "attained" the goal, is not "already perfect," but "I press on to make it (perfection) my own, because Christ Jesus has made me his own. Brethren, I do not consider that I have made it my own; but one thing I do, forgetting what lies behind and straining forward to what lies ahead, I press on toward the goal for the prize of the upward call of God in Christ Jesus" (3, 12–14).

We must observe that the "static" form, which Paul puts forward as model, is by no means the "office," nor is the "dynamic" factor the person who strives to realize the ideal embodied in the office. In fact, the *typos* is precisely the man Paul striving with such intensity (in contrast to the other persons in the ministry who "all look after their own interests, not those of Jesus Christ" [2, 21]), who in the directness of his course presents an image which is adequate and compelling. The office pure and simple with its authority Paul sees only as a last resort, a threat: I have the right, the power, in virtue of my office to demand this of you, but since I have to represent Christ to you, I do not use it (Philm. 8; 2 Cor. 13, 2. 10). It is easy to threaten with the rod of office, but those reprimanded must be induced to prefer charity to the rod: this is the art of Paul (1 Cor. 4, 21). It is, indeed, no human, personal, psychological art, but a divine one: "I was with you in weakness and fear and much trembling. And my speech and my preaching was not in the persuasive words of human wisdom, but in the showing of the Spirit and power; that your faith might not stand on the wisdom of men, but on the power of God" (1 Cor. 2, 3–5). And yet, there is no absolute cleavage between the preaching and the weakness of the man. The Spirit of God is active in both, and brings both into a unity established by him, for "we have received . . . the Spirit which is from God, that we might understand the gifts bestowed on us by God. And we impart this in words not taught by human wisdom but taught by the Spirit. . . . Yet among the mature do we impart wisdom . . . a secret and hidden wisdom of God" (2 Cor. 2, 12–13. 6. 7). It is only the combination of the two that results in the "image" to be imitated, for, were it not for his weaknesses, the foolishness, nakedness, homelessness, persecution, and calumny, the image of the crucified would not be stamped on the life of the person sent. Those holding the first place must be as "apostles, as last of all, like men sentenced to death" (1 Cor. 4, 9); otherwise, they are not images expressing Christ. For this reason, the gloss is correct which to the exhortation "be imitators of me" adds the words "as I also am of Christ" (1 Cor. 4, 16), though Paul never puts the two images on the same level. For if his own life is one marked with the form of the cross (Gal. 2, 19; Col. 1, 24), yet the voluntary, innocent suffering of Christ is beyond all comparison with the sufferings of the "first of sinners" (1 Tim. 1, 15). This contrast is always presupposed when the one is held as a reproduction and expression of the other (2 Tim. 3, 10–12), or a just parallel drawn between Christ's crucifixion "in weakness" but living "in the power of God" and Paul's being "weak in him" and living "by the power of God" (2 Cor. 13, 4).

Once again we see how Paul, so far from presuming on his official position to admonish the community for its manner of life, does just the opposite. He refers to his manner of life in order to shake them out of their certainties, of being "already filled, already become rich," already reigning (1 Cor. 4, 8). It is not by his office that the apostle represents Christ for the community, but as one humiliated in Christ, made "a spectacle to the world, to angels and to men" (v. 20). To be a person sent, one must have died and have been crucified to the world, and this must be apparent in the office. Consequently, he owes it to the office to show forth subsequently in his person this essential condition which it presupposes. If he does this, then, and only then, is the office discharged in a Christian way, and has the same theological and apologetic force both for Christians and non-Christians as the Christian's witness with his life, which, indeed, is a witness only as a dying with Christ into the new God-given form.

This makes clear the meaning of 2 Corinthians 5, 11–21, where Paul attributes the source of the official mission to the fact of dying with Christ and to the "new creature" that results. This dying with Christ is not simply to be understood sacramentally (Rom. 6, 3 f.; Col. 3, 3) as a fact, but is the outcome of the "charity which presses us," from the thought that, "if one died for all, then all were dead . . . and may not now live to themselves." This radical self-renunciation, in order "to live in Christ," means becoming "a new creature." This "new creature" is, moreover, not only a passive transference into Christ, but—since the form of Christ is imparted to us—an active sharing in him, an active reception into us of Christ's mission: "All this is from God, who through Christ reconciled us to himself and gave us the ministry of reconciliation; that is, God was in Christ reconciling the world to himself, not counting their trespasses against them, and entrusting to us the message of reconciliation. So we are ambassadors for Christ, God making his appeal through us. We beseech you on behalf of Christ, be reconciled to God. For our sake he made him to be sin who knew no sin, so that in him we might become the righteousness of God" (2 Cor. 5, 18–21).

Christ's being made sin is something over and above his person and office; it is the outcome of his perfect love and obedience to the Father, these two being identical. The Christian, the apostle, is steeped in this form of Christ and made a new creature; and in him, therefore, only one form can come into being, one that is the product of love and the ministerial office indissolubly conjoined. The "ministry of reconciliation" between God and the world can only mean the "beseeching word of reconciliation," though "the kingdom of God does not consist in speech but in power" (1 Cor. 4, 20), and, consequently, for the discharge of this embassy of Christ and collaboration with God (2 Cor. 6, 1), nothing short of total commitment of life is sufficient (6, 4–10), putting "no obstacle in any one's way, so that no fault may be found with our ministry" (6, 3). Paul lays abundant stress on the special commission given him by God, the ministerial charisma, which is passed on by the imposition of hands (2 Tim. 1, 6); and it stamps the person called to be a *typos* for the Church in that he puts his whole life at its disposal. Likewise, the First Letter of Peter makes those in the ministry a *forma gregis* in that, far from exercising it under compulsion or by compelling others, they are, like Peter himself, "witnesses of the sufferings of Christ," which means two things: presence, as betrayer and bitterly repentant, at Christ's Passion, and witness thereto by his own passion (1 Pet. 5, 1–4).

This life of bearing witness is as unique in Christianity and beyond rational analysis as is the mystery of Christ himself. In this aspect, the form of life of Paul and of every Christian is just as much an article of faith (part of the *credo Ecclesiam*) as are those concerning Christ. But the official character of the apostle and his disciple is no harder to accept than the possibility of the Christian form of life in general. As Paul is *typos* for the communities, so are the communities of Judaea *typos* for those of Thessalonica (1 Thess. 1, 7). Nor does either consciously aim at "exemplarity," for "it is required of stewards [only] that they be found trustworthy," neither judging themselves nor caring how others judge them (1 Cor. 4, 3). The Christian does not belong to himself, but to God and the Church, and only so is he *typos* and "fellow workers of God" (1 Cor. 3, 9). In himself he is nothing, merely a "servant"

(1 Cor. 3, 5; 4, 1; 2 Cor. 4, 5). And precisely in the extent to which Christians are servants can they be fruitful, and become "fathers" of the communities (1 Cor. 4, 15; 1 Thess. 2, 7. 11). What is not capable of analysis is the relationship between surrendering what is one's own and imparting to others what is divine, wherein what is also imparted is what was surrendered and is now become new. The lover, who desires to possess nothing and gives up all he has, in fact possesses all things, and the most needy can enrich all men (2 Cor. 6, 10).

This, however, is the mystery of God in Christ himself; and, therefore, the Christian *typos* reaches out in an uninterrupted ascent from Paul to Christ and to God. He thus carries on the Gospel idea of following and imitation, supplementing, it may be, the more Jewish terminology by the more Greek one of "imitation" but preserving its content. If the Sermon on the Mount demands that Christians "be perfect, as your heavenly Father is perfect" (Mt. 5, 48), namely, in *caritas,* which makes no distinction between friend and enemy, Paul says the same, in effect, when he urges Christians to "be kind to one another, tenderhearted, forgiving one another, as God in Christ forgave you," and to "walk in love, as Christ loved us and gave himself up for us, a fragrant offering and sacrifice to God" (Eph. 4, 32—5, 2). Once again, following and imitation refer to the central disposition, to humility and gentleness, love, forgiveness, mutual reconciliation, patience in bearing with weaknesses and scandals. In such a way does Paul present the great exemplar of the Son coming down in the form of a servant, in obedience and the ignominy of the cross (Phil. 2, 1–11); so too does Romans 15, 2–7, point to Christ as a model for the "strong," who are to bear the infirmities of the weak and not to please themselves. "Welcome one another, therefore, as Christ has welcomed you, for the glory of God" (15, 7). Yet again, Paul this time adducing his own example intermediately, in 1 Corinthians (10, 32—11, 1): "Give no offense to Jews or to Greeks or to the Church of God, just as I try to please all men in everything I do, not seeking my own advantage, but that

of many, that they may be saved. Be imitators of me, as I am
of Christ."

Paul and Christ can even be conjoined with the community
as a single exemplar (1 Thess. 1, 6–7). The unity consists in having "left all things" and having taken up obediently the divine
commission. In this way, the Thessalonians can, through receiving the word in much tribulation, be themselves imitators.

Orthodox Protestantism, in contradistinction to pietism, has
always, as it does today, rejected the idea of an *imitatio* of Christ
as ignoring the distance between him and us, and tantamount to
a sacrilege. It is, however, not without interest to observe that,
in view of the mimesis texts of St. Paul, this attitude can only
be sustained, so it seems, by emphasizing the authority of the
apostolic office. For Michaelis, the *typos* is not so much the pattern to be copied as the exemplar to be followed. In Philippians
3, 17, though Paul associates himself with other "models" in the
community, he has, indisputably, a place apart, grounded in his
apostolic office. And although he puts forward his conduct as a
model, yet in the demand "Be imitators of me" he claims, above
all, obedience. It is the same, especially, in 1 Corinthians 4, 16;
likewise, in reference to this passage, also 1 Corinthians 11, 1,
and the same in 1 Thessalonians 1, 6, and Ephesians 5, 1. Even
the other passages where his quality as a pattern is given special
prominence, as 2 Thessalonians 5, 7, and Philippians 3, 17,
the factor of his authority is not to be ignored.

We do not contest this factor of authority; in fact, we are
glad that it is so frankly recognized. And it is equally clear that
Paul, when he puts himself forward as a model, only intends,
by his relationship with Christ, to lead men to the unique Lord
(2 Cor. 4, 5). He alone is the image, to which we are "conformed," according to which we are "reformed" through God's
grace and the actions of his sacraments, but also through our
coöperation in action and contemplation (Rom. 8, 29; 2 Cor.
3, 18). Paul is a "model" precisely in that he directs himself
according to the model of Christ, or rather has been directed
according to this model by God's grace which has given him the

ministry. But we are associated with him in virtue of the indissoluble unity of the Christian form of life, which is put forward by Paul as our model only because it is to be understood, not in an ethical or psychological way, but in a representative way. With the apostle in particular, and those in the ministry in general, this form has the character that belongs to the office, a character which, as a special "revelation" of the power and authority of Christ "in" the person revealed (Gal. 1, 16), appears, in actual life, as a heightened, publicly manifested, image of Christ (2 Cor. 4, 8 f.), and this precisely "for your sakes" (v. 15). This instrumental character of the apostolic life, whose humiliations are designed for the exaltation of the community, and sufferings for its consolation (1 Cor. 4, 8–10; 2 Cor. 1, 6–7), is not a mere functioning of a law of the ministry, in virtual independence; it is simply the "law" of Jesus Christ himself applied to those sent. It is a wholly personal manner of representing Christ, his being poor that we may become rich (2 Cor. 8, 9), that balance in the mystical body which is what manifests, in the social sphere, the heart of the Redeemer. Here too the law holds good according to which the ministry, far from being in contrast with personal following, in fact derives from it, is embedded in it, and that its apparent impersonality is no more than the manifestation of the Trinitarian superpersonality as a constitutive element in the Church by the will of its founder, the sphere which personal following, by the grace of God, ultimately reaches. If this were not true for the laity also, it would be impossible to understand why and how they should imitate those in the ministry and take them as their model. But as for those in the ministry, their office is so rooted in the very heart of their following that any division between ministry and life, any reliance on the functions of the ministry without personal involvement and sacrifice, can only be an affliction to Paul (Phil. 1, 15–17; 2, 20–21; 3, 18–19; 2 Tim. 4, 10–6), and therefore to Christ whom he represents (Phil. 3, 10).

All this is confirmed in the other epistles of the New Testament. That to the Hebrews makes Christians followers of all those who believed before them, and, if we take together all the examples adduced, calls faith a spiritual "leaving all things" in order to stake everything on the promise of God, "going out, not knowing where" (11, 8), "sojourning in the land of promise as in a foreign land, living in tents . . . he looked forward to the city which has foundations, whose builder and maker is God" (11, 9–10). No possessions, therefore, even in the holy land; only a prospect of a heavenly country. Considering "abuse suffered for the Christ greater wealth than the treasures of Egypt" (11, 26). "Mocking and scourging, and even chains and imprisonment (11, 36), but also overpowering of earthly contrivances: conquest of kingdoms, exercise of justice, valor in battle (11, 33–44). Thus faith is, indeed, a protective form into which man enters by leaving himself, which exposes him naked to God's loving chastisement (12, 4–11), while at the same time assuring him an impregnable fortress, armor that cannot be pierced. And always "looking to Jesus the pioneer and perfecter of our faith, who for the joy that was set before him endured the cross, despising the shame. . . . Consider him who endured from sinners such hostility against himself, so that you may not grow weary or fainthearted" (12, 2–3). Undoubtedly, here Christ himself (as in the beginning of Mark) is seen in the form of life that, with us, is called faith, even though it may be disputed whether faith is ascribed to him formally or *eminenter*. What is certain is that, by his form, he is the author and finisher of the form of faith. In chapter 13, which is certainly by Paul, and perhaps comes from a lost epistle, the leaders of the community are mentioned: "Remember your leaders, those who spoke to you the word of God; consider the outcome of their life, and imitate their faith" (13, 7). Looking to the end (*respice finem*) is what brings out the full meaning of their life as a form of faith. This is what is put forward for imitation and now expressly bound up with obedience to those in charge of souls (13, 17).

Peter's first letter places the believer straightway in the supernatural form of faith. He is "born anew to a living hope," "to an inheritance ... in heaven," through his existence in this form directed to the eschatological manifestation of salvation. Here also the prophetic existence of the old covenant is adduced as serving, and ordained to, this form of faith of the new (1, 1–12). This form requires, as in the old covenant, the reproduction in man of the holiness of God (Lev. 11, 44), walking as "obedient children" in the form of God himself, and therefore walking "in fear," all the more so as they are children redeemed by the "lamb without blemish or spot" (1, 14–19). Instead of being "fashioned" according to their former desires (1, 14), there is now "obedience for love" (1, 22); they must be "built up" into the edifice of Christ, the "chief cornerstone," and in it, through him, offer themselves as a spiritual sacrifice. This sublime form is "honor" for the obedient in faith, but a scandal to "them that believe not"; once again and finally, by this form, Hosea separates those who are the "people" from those who are "not my people." Again this form is, for the Christian, "conversation," a reality of grace, undeniable and lived, to be shown to the world, that wrongdoers "may see your good deeds and glorify God" (2, 1–12).

Obedience to secular authority must be, therefore, to calumniators (of the Christian form as an eschatological revolution), a proof of their belonging to a higher order; the Christian status of "servants of God" must be shown by their good conduct in the secular sphere (2, 13–17). In fact, submission to an inconsiderate and hard master becomes an opportunity for the servant to imitate the *forma Christi*. "For to this you have been called, because Christ also suffered for you, leaving you an example, that you should follow in his steps. He committed no sin; no guile was found on his lips. When he was reviled, he did not revile in return; when he suffered, he did not threaten; but he trusted to him who judges justly. He himself bore our sins in his body on the tree, that we might die to sin and live to righteousness. By his wounds you have been healed. For you were straying like sheep, but have now returned to the Shepherd and Guardian of your souls" (2, 21. 25).

This is perhaps the strongest passage in the New Testament

for the *imitatio Christi,* and, like those in the Gospel, brings out the paradox in all its sharpness. Since the form of the Christian in its entirety has been brought about by the sufferings of Christ, and he, in suffering unjustly, bore our sins and carried them to the cross, we ourselves were originally represented in his sufferings as those wrongdoers whom we now have to bear with in imitation of him. *In tanta similitudine major dissimilitudo.* The contrast cuts across the similarity in such a way that the more the similarity comes to the fore, the more profoundly does the contrast stamp itself on the follower of Christ. Therefore, any danger of confusion with the Redeemer is made more and more remote. Everything in our form is his, even when some merit seems to accrue to us. This is something which Peter constantly repeats in various forms. The Christian form of life for wives preaches more eloquently than the word. It is above all the "being subject," the adaptation to the form, which is for them the married state in the concrete. But the husband must also adapt himself to this ordering, since he and the woman are "joint heirs of the grace of life" (3, 1–7). All are obliged to Christian love that does not render "reviling for reviling" (3, 9), that "suffers for righteousness' sake," and thus "reverences Christ the Lord" (3, 15), him who "died for sins" (3, 18) that we, having died, might live with him through resurrection and baptism (3, 19–22). Our being exposed before the world which fails to understand our new way of life, speaking evil and persecuting us (4, 3–4) is incapable of harming us (3, 13). We are "armed," because we live in the "will of God" (4, 2; 3, 17; 4, 19; 5, 6), under whom we humble ourselves and on whom we cast all our care (5, 6–7). We are not to trouble ourselves about the form of the Christian, but be content to know that it springs from "the same thought" as the form of Christ suffering (4, 1). Consequently, each must, in serving, "administer" his particular form as Christian, his "grace," whether it be mutual charity or hospitality or the gift of speaking the word of God or a "ministry" which may be given in the power of God (4, 7–11). The "elders" should be "examples to the flock," the "young men subject" to them, both commanding and obeying in the same spirit of humility (5, 1–5). All should know that "participation in the sufferings of Christ" is a matter of "joy," in fact of "glory," the reverse of shame, and the proof of the rightness of the way, for "the time has come for judgment to begin with the household of God" (4, 12–19).

James refers not so much to the pattern of Christ as to that of the prophets and Job in their patience (Jas. 5, 10–11), but even so, from his insistence on the command of love, with its self-abasement (1, 9–10; 4, 10) and its stooping to the humbled (2, 2–8. 15–17), the image of Christ clearly emerges (2, 1). If he commends action (1, 25; 2, 14–26), he mainly stresses meekness and patience (1, 3. 20–21; 3, 13. 17; 4, 1; 5, 7–11), which includes restraining the tongue (1, 26; 3, 1–12); and this is simply to adapt oneself to the form freely engendered by God, coming down from him as a good and perfect thing (1, 17–18). Like the Old Testament wisdom, it can only be prayed for (1, 5–7), in a spirit of detachment from possessions, since these are the greatest hindrance to entrance into the form of God (4, 13—5, 6).

For John, this form is simply the eternal love between the divine Persons, and therefore hardly comprehensible as "form." Yet the dialectic of the transition from one's own existence (in sin and the confession of sin—1 Jn. 1, 8–9) to the forgiveness of sins (1, 9; 2, 12; 3, 5) and rebirth out of God to sinlessness (3, 9) enables us to see the actual becoming of the form. The act of love is the essential thing, as in James 3, 17; but only when it proceeds from "abiding," and therein persists, does it have its source in the form of God (3, 6). Whoever loves has knowledge, and whoever keeps the word is in charity (2, 3–5; 3, 6). All this is the echo of the being and conduct of Christ. For God first loved us (4, 19), and sent his Son into the world as a propitiation for our sins, that we might live through him (4, 9–10). We are, therefore, already inserted into love, and so it is only obedience to the reality and not our own

93

achievement if we let what God has done in us through Christ be verified by acting accordingly. "Beloved, if God so loved us, we also ought to love one another" (4, 11). "By this we know love, that he has laid down his life for us; and we ought to lay down our lives for the brethren" (3, 16). "He who says he abides in him ought to walk in the same way in which he walked" (2, 6). All this is, indeed, a "commandment" (3, 22–24; 5, 2–3; 2 Jn. 6), but it is more, since it is Christ's dwelling in us. The Spirit given to us (2, 20–28; 3, 9; 3, 24—4, 2; 4, 13; 5, 6–8) makes us God's children, who must also love his eternal Son (5, 1–2).

All these variations on the single theme of following Christ reproduce the same motive, which continues always in the clear-cut form it had in the beginning, and whose mysterious riches will never be exhausted. The first leap of faith which leaves all things is never over and done with; it remains a constant determinant of the form, and enters into it; and the humility of Christ can only be our form by our being continuously humbled on account of our having caused the humiliation of Christ. Only in this way can Paul go almost to the point of assimilating himself to Christ, and ascribe to the individual Christian in his sufferings (as distinct from the Church as a whole) a share is the expiatory power of the passion (Col. 1, 24). Only thus can Christian love, which destroys the self in order to build up the whole body, be thought of as participating in the fruitfulness of Christ and in his self-renunciation (Eph. 4, 16). Without this working of the Spirit of Christ in the members, *purely* through the objective, sacramental, and official mode of action, nothing in the body of Christ is built up and established. The whole objective and official element is simply the substructure and means to bring forth the subjective form of Christ in each Christian.

5. HISTORICAL SKETCH

The history of Christian ideas consists in the perpetually renewed attempt to follow Christ's commands and example, to understand his design and his commission, to explain them and make them fruitful for each succeeding age. The Gospel always remains and so does man, the sinner and the hearer of its message. Its exposition, however, may vary in two ways. It may proceed from within, from the Holy Spirit who explains Christ to the Church and shows ever new aspects of his person and doctrine. Or it may proceed from the historical situation, which also throws new light on these, and may involve new demands on the Church and the Christian. It is thus possible that interpretations varying according to the time and the particular emphasis may yet meet at the center, just as different transverse sections of an object may all pass through the center. They will be consistent with one another only insofar as they actually make contact with the center and radiate forth from it, and insofar as, despite their external differences, they are ultimately in affinity. It is hard to make the temporal developments fit into a rational scheme (such as Hegel did for world history). Even should the sequence of external events be brought within a scheme which elucidates them, the designs of the Spirit, who breathes where he will, cannot be wholly perceived and ordered this side of eternity. The temporal significance and direction which is undoubtedly present and must be assumed can only be divined here and there.

1. The first period of the idea of the following of Christ is characterized by the fact of martyrdom. This was brought to bear by the persecution of Christians, together with the expectation of the imminent end of all things, as also by the tenor of the apostolic writings, many of which (Thessalonians, Philippians, Hebrews, 1 Peter, the letters in Revelation, among others) were written to fortify men under persecution, and others composed under the threat of martyrdom (the prison letters, 2 Peter, those to Timothy, Titus and Philemon, 3 John). It is but a step from these to Ignatius of Loyola. The apostles had, in fact, not produced any detailed commentary on the words of Christ, but only explained, with astonishing freedom and independence,

the meaning and import of Christ, of his death and resurrection. Certainly, his words and miracles were also recorded, but the main point of the kerygma consisted in his death and resurrection. And this was the focal point for the Christian; here was the sphere in which he had to follow Christ. The response of the Church in martyrdom was the best and most literal that could be conceived. But although the liberal interpretation may have been the *typos* and the compelling example for all Christians, the right response of the time, it was not applicable to all times and conditions.

2. Even before the persecutions ceased, the need was felt, in the third century, to adopt a position vis-à-vis the religious culture of the time. The incarnate *Logos* became the true *sophia* or *gnosis,* and following him in love, by overcoming the passions (*apatheia*) became the true philosophy. The Greek and Gnostic idea of negation of the world through spiritual ascent and turning away from the finite through imitation of the divine life was confronted by Christian virginity as a positive response. Philo had already fashioned the synthesis between the Greek "following of God" (Pythagoras, Plato, Epictetus) and the biblical "walking in the ways of God," as also with the late-Judaistic imitation of the attributes of God. It is extremely difficult, if not impossible, to say where, in the theology and spirituality of the Alexandrians and Cappadocians, the ancient Platonism and Stoicism is simply used as a means of expression and where Christian thought (though it involved some limitation upon its life-giving paradox) is made subservient to the ideas of the time. Both trends can be present in one and the same thinker; beneath the far-reaching adaptations and concessions, there may often enough lie concealed a genuine Christian integrity. It is much the same with the great heresies of the time, Gnosticism and Arianism, which on the one hand brought out the true nature of Catholicism, and on the other not seldom compelled the emergence within it of an antithesis more or less

dependent on them. Does the mystery of the cross really find a central place in Origen's system? Is his wholehearted idea of the following of Christ perhaps of a too ascetical nature, a necessary training for the perfect mastery of the gnosis; and is this not also the case with the struggle against the devils on behalf of the Churches taught by the *Didascalia?* We may ask, also, if with him, and Methodius, Gregory of Nyssa, even Ambrose and Augustine, the idea of virginity is wholly free from the spiritualism of late antiquity, and whether the "following of God" with its bold paradoxes in the "life of Moses" of Gregory of Nyssa is really the continuation of the Gospel following of Christ and of the Old Testament walking in the way of God. Even with the great St. Antony, who started such a genuine Christian movement, when he took so literally the command to "leave all things," we may wonder if going into the desert, with such exclusive emphasis on the inner life, was not a restriction of the Christian ethic to a single aspect of it. At all events, the desert spirituality, bound up with that of neighboring Alexandria, could easily shift the idea of the following of Christ onto a sidetrack, with the consequent risk, not so much of forthright errors, but—though fought against by a prudent discernment of spirits—of being misled by the contact of Christianity with the Asiatic world religions. Evagrius—from whom the way leads directly to Mount Athos and Palamitism, and indirectly, through Palladius and Cassian, to Western monasticism —aimed, through the renunciation of all images and concepts, to attain to the inner light of the soul, and through it to the divine light of grace, in which, ultimately, the uncreated Trinitarian light of the Father might itself shine forth. Even Augustine was deeply involved in the Asiatic approach of the neo-Platonists, and only by degrees found the way from a religious philosophy with Christian affinities to a genuine theology of following the cross. On the whole, the idea of following was alien to Hellenism. The personal master-and-disciple relationship of classical philosophy had long since become obsolete, and there remained the "imitation" of God, the theory of prototype and copy with the ascent by contemplation from faith to vision.

Nevertheless, the passing of antiquity saw the emergence of a Christian form embodying all the Greek and Roman thought-forms, one that continued as the definitive, almost the sole form actuating the medieval Church. The Benedictine rule, whose mysterious author, so hard to depict historically, is revealed, in his unparalleled influence down the ages, as a formative Christian force of the highest potency, unites charisma and ministry, authority and love, zeal and discretion, the Roman and Christian character, in such a way as to be practically a model for all Christian discipleship. It is a model that did not set itself up as a rival to the Gospel, one that remained so open in its readiness to serve, that it could be developed in all directions, in the holiness of the hierarchical ministry and of personal asceticism, in missionary activity and in the stability of contemplation, in the life devoted to the liturgical *opus Dei* and in a Christian humanism in the tradition of antiquity. It is the moderate and mature super-personality of the Benedictine form that enabled it not only to produce out of itself almost all subsequent forms of monasticism, but to set its mark, directly or indirectly, on Catholic culture at all levels right up to modern times.

3. With the onset of the Germanic era the tendency was reversed. Young nations, divided up into small tribes, were naturally familiar with the idea of following and trusting the leader, and a connection was easily established between the march of the Jews through the desert and the wandering of the nations. The ethos of the "Heliand" was at great pains to distinguish this secular loyalty from the loyalty of faith of the apostles to their leader, Christ. The transposition, which in some respects was almost too easily achieved, came up against extraordinary difficulties in others, as in the providential betrayal by Peter and the flight of the disciples. Nonetheless, it was achieved, and the great preacher-poet was able to persuade his

hearers that Peter had to undergo the shame of felony for the sake of his subsequent office and the knowledge of human weakness. All through the Middle Ages the ethos of personal following prevailed, and the more it was impregnated with the Christian spirit the more marvelous were its fruits. But the two ideas were so close that they were not always sufficiently distinguished, and noble actions inspired by the secular idea were often too hastily taken as Christian in essence. In the tragedy of the Crusades, in the subtle tension between St. Louis and his follower de Joinville, in the story of Parsifal and the Arthurian tales in general, we can see both the similarities and differences in all their varieties. From the consecration of the sword and the initiation of the knight to the ceremony of anointing the king, we can see how the secular relationships of leader and follower were sacramentalized; even at so late a date, the Pope sent a consecrated sword to Charles of Lorraine and Prince Eugene. St. Ignatius raised this idea to a wholly spiritual plane in his contemplation "De Regno Christi," which set its distinctive stamp on the spirituality of his Society. Apart from the secularized Teutonic order, this is practically the only place where the idea has persisted up to the present.

4. The movement towards poverty that broke out among the Christian people was contemporary with the feudal world and (in a hidden fashion) a part of it; it began long before Francis, and, in its origin, was a reaction against the rich and princely Church: it lay on the fringe of orthodoxy. What the "poor men of Christ" longed for, from Robert of Arbrissel, Joachim, Norbert, Arnold of Brescia, and the Waldensians onwards, was direct contact with the Christ of apostolic times, the literal acceptance of the idea of "leaving all things," which had almost disappeared under the pomp of the Church's representatives. Francis brought the movement from the fringe right into the center of the Gospel. His second Rule brought together all the texts on the following of Christ under the idea of poverty, in

which the stress was laid on this following, poverty being the sign of the will's firm resolve. But for him poverty was not only a means and an expression, but a real end, since Christ willed and had to be poor to redeem us, poor in order to show us to the Father as utterly destitute. If the spirituals departed again from the center to the fringe of orthodoxy, it was still the spiritual school of the *Poverello,* the spiritualization of his idea of poverty, that became the spring of modern spirituality. Franciscan poverty was conjoined, in Bonaventure, with the "becoming nought" of the Areopagite. He was followed in this by Eckhart or Tauler, of whom the latter was a decisive influence on Spanish mysticism and also on that of France in the *grande siècle.* Poverty of life and of the spirit as the following of Christ was the constant ideal of the Brethren of the Common Life, of the *devotio moderna,* which produced Erasmus. He attempted, by the methods of philology, to bring about a rebirth of the pure Gospel and the primitive Christian tradition. In so doing, by skillfully by-passing both the Reformation and the Counter-Reformation, he founded what Friedrich Heer has christened the Third Force.

5. The idea of "following" never managed to establish itself in Luther's mind; it was cramped by his too narrow idea of faith. Yet he better than anyone else could have finally Christianized the Germanic idea of discipleship, and freed it from all accretions. He might also have liberated the Franciscan heritage, present in German mysticism, from all neo-Platonic coloring, and handed it on to the new age. Neither of these things happened. His *fiducia,* and essential element in both the Old and New Testament faith, remained isolated (and so was controverted, instead of being absorbed through a right understanding, by the Counter-Reformation idea of faith). The Christian paradox of Tauler's mysticism could not, in fact, be preserved in the Lutheran dialectic. In the late Middle Ages there was a growing rift between the institutional Church and the Church of the

personal interior life with its practice of mysticism and poverty, but now the two broke completely apart, and it became quite impossible to envisage any origin for the Church's ministry in the personal following of Christ. Consequently, after all sorts of compromises had been tried within Protestantism in the course of its history, the final victory was bound to lie with the upholders of the personal inner life. These were the most powerful figures. In this connection, we may mention Pascal and his image of Christ, since he was so strongly affected by the Jansenist doctrine of predestination; and Kierkegaard, whose assault on the liberal pastorate was the fulfillment of his life and work.

Even the Counter-Reformation was divided, more deeply than appears at first, by two contrasting trends. Its apologetics upheld the Church as a hierarchical structure, and the great saints of the Baroque era were certainly a proof of its truth; a triumphant architectural style was used to glorify both at the same time. But, as in the late Middle Ages, the true spirituality followed other, more hidden ways; it was concerned with the individual who, in his following of Christ, sought and realized the "kingdom of God within" (Lk. 17, 21) by "interior prayer." Since, however, this was pursued with a kind of mystical directness—we have only to think of Berulle's teaching on the reproduction of the "interior states" of Jesus—it did not, in fact, any longer convey the Christian "inner form." Form became exterior representation, in opposition to inwardness (the two are, more or less, embodied in the opposition between Bossuet and Fenelon). For that reason, psychology gained the upper hand, the description and scrutinizing of the mystical and other states, and the Christian commission was seen as a step, not without danger, in the direction of exteriority (Lallemant). The Catholic romantic movement, also, was dominated by the idea of inwardness. Hence it is that a little book, the *Imitation of Christ,* was so important at that time and during the subsequent period. Hence, too, the rescue from oblivion of German mysticism, and the emphasis, where the Church was

101

concerned, laid on community of love in the Holy Spirit. Twen-
tieth-century personalism continues along these lines, though it
is primarily the product of Protestantism (Kierkegaard) and
of Old Testament Judaism (Scheler, Buber). "Form" as impersonal is here seen as pertaining to the "office" or to the religious life in its ordered claustral form, and over against it
stands the life of the laity as "personal"—an opposition which,
carried to its conclusion, can only destroy Church unity, as it
has already done once.

This rough and ready account brings out clearly how the
different epochs emphasized different things, which all meet in
the center of the Gospel, but since none of them actually constitutes this center, especially when the first impulse weakens,
the outcome is a lack of balance. Christian antiquity obviously
put the accent on virginity. With Tertullian there was a clear
basis in eschatology for this, but from the Alexandrians on,
there was a Platonic motive: a spiritual way of life seen as a
condition for contemplation. It would be wrong to exaggerate
this onesidedness. The patristic treatises on virginity are thoroughly imbued with the spirit of the Gospel, profound and
stirring. Nor is it the literal following of the counsels that
brought a onesided attitude, but the adoption of motives of
flight from the world, and of a too negative asceticism. These
were already perceived by St. Augustine as bishop: if the kingdom of God is not of this world, is then, perhaps, the desert
also not of this world?

The medieval cult of poverty is admirable and astonishing for
its thoroughness, but here too, we may say that its weakness lay
precisely in its strength, in its liberal fashion of following
Christ. Francis was fully conscious that what mattered was the
heart and the spirit prompting it. For him, freedom from all
earthly goods and ties was what characterized the bride who
leaves all, who is betrothed, not to poverty, but to the divine
bridegroom in the common possession of poverty. Yet it was
the literal acceptance of poverty, combined with the "literal"
sharing of the stigmata, that was responsible for the distortions

of the Franciscan theology of discipleship and imitation, increasing in volume from the *Tractatus* of Salimbene to that of Bartholomew of Pisa—designated by Luther as the monks Eulenspiegel and Alkoran—who discovered, one by one, all the qualities of Christ perfectly mirrored in Francis, set up by the spirituals as the new spiritual man and founder of the third age of the Church. The transference of the idea of poverty on the spiritual plane, effected by the Dominican mystics, freed it from this onesidedness and restored it to the center. Rightly understood, they could say a great deal to us today.

For Ignatius, following Christ is essentially obedience, but the obedience of the feudal relationship as continued in the Spanish ideas of kingship and knighthood, as he knew it in his youth bound up with the late medieval love-service. With him, this idea of discipleship became interiorized, personal, corresponding to the new age just beginning: the vow of fidelity is the response befitting the noble heart when it contemplates the life of our Lord. The *Spiritual Exercises* proceed by way of encounter between Christ and the individual, leading up to the crucial point where his allegiance to Christ is placed at the service of the Church's hierarchy. When the pope, as the supreme head of the Society, commands any mission, this is seen and accepted as the direct command of Christ. This is personal obedience subordinated to the Church's ministry, self-renunciation carried to the utmost: magnificent indeed, but always liable to shift from the attitude of loyalty and discipleship into an impersonal striving. This is, in fact, what occurred in the collapse of the German knighthood idea into the Prussia of the Hohenzollerns and of the Kantian imperative.

For Ignatius, then, obedience as the central attitude of the Church as bride of Christ is the true core, the most sublime concept of discipleship: *ecce ancilla*. But obedience, once detached from this inner disposition (perhaps more through the one who gives, than the one who receives the commands), and seen simply as a tool for the use of the hierarchy as such, can and must lead to abuses. These are utterly remote from the con-

103

ception of the founder, who, with all his realism, always held firmly to the ideal aspect of the Church; but it is a danger still to be reckoned with on account of the hidden cleavage, already described, in the post-Reformation Church. Nonetheless, Ignatius, more than anyone else, succeeded in passing on to the present age the Gospel idea of discipleship as a living reality. He has done so in that he neither takes for criterion the person of the follower, nor lets it be wholly merged in the function. Instead, he has always in view the higher center of the living Christian form, which takes hold of the person (according to the "journey to the hell of self-knowledge" of the First Week) for the service of the Lord, and thereby secures for him true freedom.

6. DIFFICULTIES RESOLVED

We can now consider the three difficulties enunciated at the beginning, and see how they can be resolved. The solution, it is true, is only accessible to those who are ready to go so deeply into the root of the matter that the unity of all its factors emerges of itself. This unity lies in God rather than in the Church, since the unity of the latter lies not in itself, but in the Head. The Church is a manifold of members, which both differentiates it from the Head and slackens the bond between the two. "Now there are varieties of gifts, but the same Spirit; and there are varieties of service, but the same Lord; and there are varieties of working, but it is the same God who inspires them all in every one" (1 Cor. 12, 4–6).

The gifts, service, and working of each individual are not these individuals themselves; they are the "form" or "function" in the living organism of the Church imparted to each one. "All these are inspired by one and the same Spirit, who apportions to each one individually as he wills" (*ibid.*, v. 11). There is no member of the Church who, precisely *qua* member, does not have his "member-form," and this is something common to all "gifts, service, and workings." In fact, the qualities of member and member-form are strictly identical. The eye, ear, and foot, which Paul adduces in comparison, are not some sort of neutral entities who accidentally take on the function of seeing, hearing, and walking. They *are* this function which, in order to be itself, is materialized in a definite corporeal structure. In Christ, whose body we constitute, is materialized a distinct function of the human person, proclaimed by him in the Holy Spirit. This function, viewed apart from the body of Christ, may indeed be specified as part of the order of creation, but as this particular function it is related as matter to the form given by Christ in the Holy Spirit. "For by one Spirit we were all baptized into one body—Jews or Greeks, slaves or free— and were all made to drink of one Spirit" (*ibid.*, v. 13), the Spirit that has made us functions of the unity. We can see at once that this idea of function has nothing in common with modern functionalism, which presupposes the depersonalizing of the individual harnessed to his task. The totality whose functions the baptized become is not an industrial or administrative collective, but the person Jesus Christ, divine and human, in his function of revealing and imparting the triune personal life of God. Consequently, functionalizing the person baptized into Christ can only mean elevating his isolated created personality into the state and wholly new setting of the divine life so revealed and communicated. This mysterious operation becomes at once evident when we look at the actual "functioning" of the Church, for where is the human person more "holy," more redeemed, than in the place where he attains to holiness? Consider Paul, Augustine, Bernard, Teresa: all the power and energy of their personalities we see developed far beyond their natural potential. At the same time, this happened in the complete renunciation of self, in leaving all things and "hatred of self" (Lk. 14, 26). Everything about them became the expression and active functioning of God in the Church, and only in this higher setting is it comprehensible and explicable.

Once again, it is to our shame that Protestant theology had to recall us Catholics to this biblical functionalism, and so re-

105

store to us the ultimate foundation of the Church ministry. Oscar Cullmann's *Christology of the New Testament,* based on Karl Barth's idea of revelation in his *Church Dogmatics* (vol. 1, part 1), shows how the chief titles of Christ—prophet, servant of Yahweh, high priest, messiah, Son of man, Kyrios, redeemer, even Logos and Son of God—express what God wills to be in his work of saving the world. In opposing an exaggerated actualism that would merge God's Trinitarian being into his act of revelation (seeing him solely as revealer)—*esse sequitur agere*—both Barth and Cullmann emphasize the fact that we attain to God's being-in-itself only by means of his action-for-us, and that the Bible offers no possibility of framing a doctrine of God's being-in-itself in abstraction from his working in the order of revelation, even though, in the function, the person as such is always manifest as its prerequisite. One can only agree with those who are still wary of interpreting the biblical data in the Greek terminology of Nicea, Ephesus, and Chalcedon, provided that it is always realized that the conciliar formulas were intended to preserve the full import of these. Protestants undoubtedly exaggerate the contrast between the biblical-Hebraic and Greek mode of thought with its generalized philosophical approach; they view philosophy only in its most arid scholastic form. The fact is, however, that one can only frame a constructive philosophy of being in the categories of actuality, and natures cannot be understood otherwise than as sources of acts (*natura est principium actum*), form only explained in relation to its finality (though this is not to be taken in the narrow, technical sense of the Enlightenment), and to the being of the thing itself (*esse sequitur formam*).

Christ, as the Father's Word sent and incarnate, passes over from the *"forma Dei"* in which he abides, into the *"forma Servi."* Paul throws further light on the idea by the two additional terms "image" (which does not mean "similarity," but sameness of form), and "shape" (which likewise refers to form, in fact to the living form of expression, character, conduct). Thereby he indicated the inward character and the depth

OFFICE IN THE CHURCH

of the form assumed. It is no mere external way of acting, a sort of disguise, while inwardly, in character and being, one remains something quite different. On the contrary, the principle itself from which the acts issue has the form of a slave, is actually man, and the humiliation is precisely the passing over from being in the one actual form to being in the other; and so the mystery of Christology consists precisely in this "passing over," which means more than a simple addition of a second nature to a first. It would be no humiliation if, in passing over to the being of a slave, he ceased to be God; but the entrance on the form of a slave must nonetheless be seen as a real movement, an event for him too, a becoming and an "emptying" (Phil. 2, 5–8).

It is by analogy to what Christ did in descending that the Christian ascent, wrought by this descent from the "shape of man" into the form of a member of the Church, must be understood, even if there is no question of any structural identity with the hypostatic union. But what Christ is by nature we must be, through him, by grace; and, as he is wholly the "man-for-others" (Karl Barth), his person as Redeemer being wholly given over to the function of redeeming, so the redeemed human person must become, through its being made a member in Christ, a function in the mystical body. Here we must distinguish between a temporal aspect of the Church's existence, which lasts to the final judgment and the fulfillment—the only thing of which we have exact knowledge—and the eternal aspect of the Church's being, of which we are only given an intimation. In the temporal aspect, not only the individual in the Church is to be understood functionally; the Church as a whole retains, as regards the entire world to be redeemed, a functional aspect. The Church is, at one and the same time, the redeemed world in course of becoming and Christ's instrument for the full redemption of the world. Consequently, the individual member of the Church in time is not, actually, functional as regards the Church, as if it were the executive bearer of this function. He is, rather, functional in and with the

107

Church as a whole. His being as function is the expression of his being as part of the Church, and the bearer and executor of the function is plainly Christ, indeed the Trinity: "You are the body of Christ, and individually members of it" (1 Cor. 12, 27)—not then members of the Church, but members of Christ. The function-being of the Church (and of the individual members), far from excluding the personal life as an end in itself, actually includes it, so much so that it remains the indispensable center of activity, as is shown in the chapter on charity (1 Cor. 13) that follows the one about functions (1 Cor. 12); for charity fills all functions, not as if they were something disparate to it, but as its own living organs, distinct one from the other.

We are now in a position to answer the questions broached in the beginning. The most important insight, which conditions all the others, is that of the functional and representative character of the Christian form of existence, in which the human opposition between person and function is no longer applicable. For this reason, any ecclesiology which is based on this opposition, and, for instance, assigns what is personal to the laity and what is functional to the clergy, starts from a false premise. Though the cleric has a function that the layman has not, yet functionality on the Christian plane applies no less to the layman than to the cleric. At the most, it could be said that the functional character of the Church as a whole (and so of all its members) is more clearly shown in the cleric than in the layman, and that in the cleric it has its own functional character more visibly presented. The recollection of this fact is one of the sources of anti-clericalism, just as Paul's stress on himself as *typos* earned him little sympathy in the Christian communities.

Our first conclusion offers no difficulty. The question raised was whether the training of the apostles, in the Gospel, was a training for the clerical state (in which case it has no direct concern with laity), or for the Christian life in general (and then the inner connection of Orders and jurisdiction with this training is no longer clear). But the question, in view of all that has been said, is wrongly posed, since it is not a matter of alternatives, but of an inner and necessary unity. Christ trains the disciples (as also the people) in the Christian form, which as such is beyond the distinction of clergy and laity. But this common possession is not to be confused with the Protestant idea that the priesthood of all believers is the foundation of the special state of the clergy, in that the powers inherent, collectively and democratically, in the Church are imparted by it to individuals. The hierarchy, as is clear in the texts, was directly established by Christ, and is not to be referred, for its special commission, causally to anything universal in the Church. This does not rule out that the functional side of this special commission may be a particular expression of the universal function-form of the Church. Consequently, what is special is not something added, externally and positivistically, to what is universal. It is, rather, a special imprinting by Christ on the universal form, whereby it can and should be, in a more special way, *typos,* model, and pattern of this universal.

The second conclusion follows equally naturally. It is quite true that faith, in the scriptural sense, presupposes as basic principles leaving all and hating all, for anyone to be a disciple of Christ at all. It is also true that this faith, demanded of everyone, represents the human contribution to the God-given form which is sanctity. And so it follows that the so-called ordained state, or better, the religious state, which achieves in fact this leaving all according to the counsel of Christ, can, once again, be nothing else than the special manifestation of what is implied in the general state of the believer, whether this be exemplified by a layman in the world or by a cleric. Granted that the literal leaving of all things (external goods, bodily fruitfulness, and spiritual disposition over oneself) results, in the Christian setting, from a special call of Christ, yet this "special" call itself, like the response to it, is analogously present in the general Christian form of life. It is no more a question of identifying the function of Christian holiness simply with this specialized call (as if only those in the clerical or religious state were canonizable) than of denying outright the inner connection between specialized holiness and the specialized call. It is indeed obvious that this external leaving all things is the prerequisite willed by God for a man to devote his life undividedly to the service of God's kingdom (inside and outside the Church). But holiness, both general and special (and the distinction is, obviously, not a hard and fast one) exists only as a form bestowed. The religious state, therefore, is not to be valued according to the degree of subjective striving (which may be just as great, or greater, in secular state), but primarily in respect of the meaning and scope of the mission imparted, to which, admittedly, one's personal endeavor ought to correspond. The final proof of all this is St. Paul's membership theory, according to which higher qualifications (and personal distinctions) directly signify higher types of function (which means service for the whole body, especially the "weaker members") —1 Corinthians 12, 21–26. Laymen who object to the greater honor shown by the Church to religious and clerics might well reflect on these verses.

The third point at issue was that between the idea of a "personal Church" and a "peoples' Church." Indeed, the more personal and distinctive calling, with the more personal and distinctive response of the one called to his vocation (whatever form it takes), brings about a correspondingly greater isolation, makes him more independent in his missionary role, placed, as he is, in the front line of the kingdom of God. The graces of confirmation have brought a man to his full stature as a Christian when he is able to represent the faith uncompromisingly before the world, not merely before his fellow Christians. For this reason, the Church is always, in her *potior pars,* her special quality as Church, a missionary Church, a Church of witness and of martyrdom. With all that, she does not cease to be a community, but one of a very special sort; basically a centrifugal community (going apart, as it were, precisely in that which unites her, in Christ's missionary call), in contrast with the synagogue, which always as today (in Israel) has been a centripetal community, and is only missionary *per accidens*. Accordingly, the question is where we are to place the center of the Church: whether in her spiritual locus which, however, is necessarily embodied in a minority, or where by far the greatest number is to be found, though they certainly do not embody her pure idea in the clearest fashion.

At the present time, we are able to look back on the history of the following of Christ almost from an eschatological plane, and formulate a doctrine accordingly. It is a doctrine that, so far from preventing, actually stimulates us to seek and find a form of Christian discipleship relevant to the time and its spirit, which, in the light of the various attempts in the course of history, will avoid, as far as is humanly possible, any onesided and materialistic conception. The forms developed in history may correspond, afterwards as before, to special vocations, which—for instance, the purely contemplative life—are theologically as appropirate now as in times when they were more consonant with the existing culture. But, in addition, there is something like a form in the *kairos* of the present time, a form which seems given when the Christian tries to live in the world and in a secular calling a specialized Christian vocation along the lines of the Christian counsels. In this he will be, for all states of the Christian life, a specialized witness to the general form of sanctity which is the basis of all Christian living.

3.

WHO IS THE CHURCH?

1. FIGURE AND MYTH

To frame the question in this way is to presuppose that the Church is "someone," in other words a person. A person, however, seems definable only as a spiritual center of consciousness of free and rational acts. How, then, can the Church be a person in this sense? We are, of course, wont to attribute to the Church all kinds of acts: the Church wills this and that, rejoices, suffers, permits one thing or another, commands, forbids; above all she prays, thanks, intercedes, hopes, sacrifices, and, as regards men, she instructs, admonishes, feeds them. In a number of these cases, the average Christian has in mind the ecclesiastical hierarchy, which in its activities represents, at least in his eyes, the Church, if it does not exactly coincide with her. In other cases, he sees expressions of the general life of the Church, or perhaps rather expressions of her life which, while elucidated and transmitted by the hierarchy, must ultimately be ascribed, not to the latter, but to the Church in general as their subject. And so the question emerges anew: How is this general subject to be understood?

The most obvious course is to explain it as a collective subject, in the same sense as the natural groups, family, race, people, state, mankind are said to be subjects, and so we predicate of them certain acts and relationships. There is good reason to

112

designate, as is often done, collective subjects as real and not merely figurative persons, since a family, say, or a people, is essentially more than the sum of its members. Yet, since a people possesses no center of consciousness of its own, but at most one that is made up of the centers of the individual persons, one may well hold that there is merely an analogy between the individual and collective persons. We can, therefore, clarify the issue by asking whether the subject Church can be subsumed under the category of collective person, and whether we are to understand statements about it in the same way as statements as "The people wills," or "The state declares." Even in these cases the collective act is posited, or at any rate made public, by a group, large or small, of responsible individuals, such that the relationship of these to the whole body is susceptible of many gradations, from democracy to absolutism. A government may consider itself more as the expression of the collective will and feeling (though it can never be absolutely this), or else the people may agree to accept the dispositions of the government as the expression of its own attitude, and so to follow them out and comply with them.

However the relationship between the principle and the consequences may vary, some such relationship must always be present. But, as regards the Catholic Church, when we look more closely, no secular form of constitution can be predicated of it. It is true that, externally, it seems to have a pronounced monarchic and aristocratic constitution that attributes all initiative to the pope and the bishops holding office *jure divino,* and is by no means representative of the "will of the people." At the same time, however, these rulers are "believers" equally and in the same sense as all the rest. They do not follow their own will, not even representing anything like a spiritual *"raison d'état,"* but discharge their office in absolute dependence on the real supreme Head of the Church. This Head is the glorified Christ, his person transcendent over the whole Church, sovereign and unaccountable. For him it is no sort of hubris, but a simple statement of fact, to make the equation: *L'Eglise, c'est moi.*

If we take this literally, we already have the answer to the

113

question "Who is the Church?" The subject of the Church is, then, simply Christ; he posits and is responsible for her acts in the sense of St. Augustine's reiteration against the Donatists: It is not Peter who baptizes, nor Paul, nor Judas, but Christ alone. We can see, then, why we feel the inappropriateness of making the Church one of a number of "collective persons." No collective, in the secular order, can be in this way referred to an individual subject, so as to take its origin therefrom and be so utterly dependent on it. The Church, however, is "Christ living on"; she is, to use Paul's great simile, *Christ's body*. This means, if we allow its full range of meaning, that the Church, in regard to her Head, is not a person on her own, a new and second one. The "body," in the sense of the simile, forms, together with the "Head," one being, that is, she is a person only "by grace" of the "Head."

It is not part of the nature of the Head, in Paul's simile, to need a body in order to be a person. Christ, being God, has no need of a Church. But it is absolutely of the essence of this body that it should need this Head, in order to participate in his personality, and, in that way, to be a body at all. The entire "organism" that the Church forms, and as which Christ willed her to be and founded her, together with its hierarchical structure and monarchical apex, is, taken by itself, headless, acephalous. The consciousness or self-awareness ascribable to it as to a secular corporation, is far from being that intended for it in reality, and which it ought to possess and, in fact, does possess, because it is poured into it by Christ. The verse of the psalm,

> *. . . it is like the precious oil upon the head,*
> *running down upon the beard,*
> *upon the beard of Aaron* [*133, 2*],

was, for the Fathers, an eloquent image of the grace flowing down in abundance from the Head onto the body, which owes this grace, preëminently, its participation in the personality of Christ.

The simile of a body answers the question "Who is the

114

Church?" only in a negative sense; she is, and cannot be other than, an extension, a communication, a partaking of the personality of Christ. This is comprehensible in some degree only if Christ is seen as both God and man. He became so as to be of the same nature as we are and so to be our Head, and this in order to impart to us, through his humanity, the Trinitarian life he shares as God. We cannot, then, stop, at Christ's self-consciousness, for this, as human, cannot be set apart and understood in isolation from his divine consciousness, which includes the whole Trinitarian consciousness. Thence grace, as participation in the divine life, flows into the Church, through the mediation of Christ, grace which has its own "consciousness" in the divine virtues of faith, hope, and charity. These three are personal spiritual dispositions which impart an essential "life" of God, but one that is conscious, though for the time being still veiled, and disclosed in its full "consciousness" only in the world beyond. "Life," when predicated of God, in St. John and Scripture generally, means nothing "biological." It is used to express the whole intimacy and intensity of the divine thinking, feeling, and willing.

This applies also to the simile of the vine, in which the "biological" element is obviously an expression of both the ontological and the personal inwardness of Christ's indwelling in the Church. The clarity of his thinking, the strength of his willing, the consistency of his love, all make up the life which flows into us from him, without which we can do nothing, but when present enables us to bring forth the awaited fruit. Here the unique principle of life dwelling in Christ is more strongly emphasized than in the simile of the body. Even when the comparison is drawn between the stock that is not seen and the fruit which is so evident, the whole achievement of the branches yet belongs to it, more clearly than in the other simile, in which the body is understood as the product and prolongation of the Head. The least tendency to independence on the part of the branches as regards the stock would be the beginning of a withering process, and lead to their being cast into the fire.

115

There is nothing fruitful in the branches that does not come from the stock, and, though unseen, really preëxist there: *Quis in Christo est omnis Ecclesia.*

The last image of this, one frequent with the Fathers, is the origin of the Church *from the wounded side* of the crucified Lord. There is no doubt that subsequent theology owes a great deal to St. John's picture of the opening of Christ's side and the flowing out of water and blood. There can be no doubt at all that, for John, water and blood represent all the sacraments, nor that the whole event, of which the presence of Mary and the beloved disciple beneath the cross forms a part, signifies the extreme of love, at once divine and human, in its self-manifestation. It is equally certain that, for John, Christ's giving up his spirit to the Father at the moment of this gift from within his body has a Trinitarian and ecclesiological sense, and is connected with the glorified Christ's gift of the Spirit at Easter. Spirit, water, and blood, in their unity, are the "three witnesses" of this unique divine and human love, and their unity has evidently to do with the inner essence of the Church. That the Church essentially originated on the cross,[1] and represents the creative achievement and outcome of the passion suffered on man's behalf, is theologically undeniable. The only question that remains is what the reality issuing from Christ's dying body was in fact: whether solely the attributes of the spirit and body of the God-man being poured forth externally in the sacramental forms—and thereby the Trinitarian grace granted to mankind in Christological form—or whether in the crucified, dying representative of humanity some element of preëxisting sinful man must be deemed present so as to be a kind of second agent coöperating in this founding and outpouring of the Church. If the latter is taken as the more consonant, then the transition from the image of the Church as body to that of the Church as bride is accomplished imperceptibly.

In the great text of Ephesians 5, the comparison between

1. Certainly, as we will show, on the cross as inseparable from the Easter event, especially as it is understood by St. John.

116

husband and wife on the one hand, and Christ and the Church on the other, obliges us to take the image of Head and body in a nuptial and personal sense. In this setting, "Head" means the ruling partner, the lord, in a marriage; "body" means completion and unification in the physical nuptial order. This transposition demands, henceforth, the maintenance together of both statements: the personal, in virtue of which the Church is a "someone" whom the Lord loved and for whom he delivered himself up, a "someone," therefore, who in a certain way already existed; and the somatic, in virtue of which the Church is what she is, namely, the glorious one without spot or wrinkle, yet owing her origin wholly to this event of the cross. The paradox, not to say contradiction, Paul could only sustain by bringing to it his prior theological understanding of the doctrine of the sexes, the origin, that is, of the first woman from the rib of man, whereby she is said to be both "his own flesh and blood" and a "person" for whose sake the man is to "leave his father and mother and cleave to his wife." And since this two-fold statement of Genesis, to which Paul refers, is inapplicable to Adam and Eve, since Adam had no parents to leave, it must have to do with the future. And so Paul, who elevates the sex relationship from type to antetype, is yet undoubtedly thinking of the simultaneous realization of both aspects in the relationship between Christ and the Church. Those Fathers who speak, in connection with Ephesians 5 and Philippians 2, of Christ leaving and coming down from the Father (and, with Origen, also from the "mother," the "heavenly Jerusalem," after Galatians 4, 26), in order to cleave to his bride in her fallen state on earth and estranged from God, simply make fully comprehensible Paul's statement that Christ loved the Church and gave himself on the cross for her; and the second explanation adopted by them is equally in accord with Paul's train of thought—the Church, purified on the cross and made glorious without spot or wrinkle, was previously lacking in such purity and splendor, and was endowed with these qualities only on the cross, in the new covenant.

There are, then, two divergent images of the Church. On the one hand, the Church is seen as originating wholly from the dying Christ; on the other, she is considered preëxisting. From these, there follow the equally divergent aspects of a Church which is no more than the outpouring and prolongation of the twofold nature of Christ, and of a Church which confronts Christ as a "someone," a subject, a person. Paul, in his tremendous vision, conjoins these seeming incompatibles; and we may well ask, seeing that the passage in Genesis did not require but merely prompted it, if he could have done so apart from the background of the contemporary mythical Gnostic way of thinking. This was prone both to personalize abstractions and also to represent the world principles in sexual terms, making them emerge from the primal source as a male-female couple. There is no need to postulate this as directly influencing the theological process, but it suffices to see it as working in the background by way of suggestion, facilitating the approach, and providing the occasion; while the inner theological treatment of the themes, once provided, proceeds independently. Thus the abundant fruits yielded by the conception of the Church as bride of Christ in the patristic age, and also in the medieval exegetes following the Fathers, are quite independent of any Gnostic prompting, and ascribable to the convergence of a great number of biblical themes. But a time came when the bride-image became blurred and lost its hold on men's minds, and this is true today for the general consciousness of the Church. The simile of the body has been resuscitated and is again in vogue, but this had not happened to the simile of the bride. The reason for this hesitation in ecclesiological thought must now be examined.

2. THE PROBLEM OF THE SCRIPTURAL BASIS

It is today generally recognized, of course, that the Genesis image, which St. Paul applied, of Eve coming forth from Adam's rib, must itself be taken as a piece of religious symbolism ("myth"). But this image, so striking and rich in theological content, ought to be the origin of the spontaneous act of hypostasizing the Church, making her the bride, a person contrasting with the divine and human bridegroom; for the image of bride, in its content, goes beyond that of the "mystical" body, though of course without contravening it. This had to be made explicit, since one might well think of a "bride" who was not, at the same time, "body," as was the case with the Old Testament Israel of Zion, God's betrothed or spouse (no essential difference for Jewish law, since the man's marriage rights were already conveyed in the betrothal, though to be exercised only after marriage). "For your Maker is your husband . . . and the Holy One of Israel is your Redeemer, the God of the whole earth he is called. For the Lord has called you like a wife forsaken and grieved in spirit, like a wife of youth when she is cast off, says your God" (Is. 54, 5–6). "Go and proclaim in the hearing of Jerusalem, Thus says the Lord, I remember the devotion of your youth, your love as a bride, how you followed me in the wilderness, in a land not sown" (Jer. 2, 2). Further, all these texts which speak of judgment, denouncing Jerusalem's adultery, enormously strengthen the realism of the image, making it operate so forcefully that one can hardly speak any longer of a mere image. In addition, these texts establish a singular continuity, little noticed in theology, between the disfigured bride of God in the old covenant and the bride of Christ in the new, expressly said to have been bathed and washed, and therefore glorious and unspotted. Later, we will go further into these correlations. For the moment, it is just a matter of seeing that Israel, as Yahweh's spouse, is indeed a kind of subject, but nothing in the nature of a "body" of God.

The physical correlation is reserved to the new covenant. Israel is, above all, God's people, and as such a collective subject, even if of peculiar constitution and value. It never saw itself in any other light—except, perhaps, in that later period when Gnosticism had already started. In fact, even at the beginning and at the zenith of its course, it saw its relation to Yahweh as analogous to that of other peoples to their God-leaders, nor did it deny the existence of their religious cov-enants, but only their lawfulness. Furthermore, we may take the whole manner of thinking of this early period to have been "mythological," for it regarded, unreflexingly, both the peoples and their gods and the hierarchies of divinities as real unities. It was a very human, realistic mode of conception, saturated with imagery, which ceded only to philosophy with its power of abstract thought, and which may well have left its mark on the simile of the marriage of Yahweh with his people. The nuptial simile, indeed, was not exclusive to Israel, but was used and misused over and over again by other peoples. Its use by Israel was distinguished from that by the neighboring cultures only in its absolute purity and severity, indeed in its predom-inantly sharp and juridical form—thought the distinction is an essential one. The exceptional case is that of the Song of Songs, though it still follows the general line in that there is never even a hint of reference to the relations between Yahweh and Israel: this is an amazing piece of discretion observed even by the latest compilers of the corpus of writings, who no doubt included it in view of its allegorical meaning. It must, then, be the case that the sensuous portrayal of the two lovers was meant to become, in the history of Christian theology, the predestined *typos* for the development of the New Testament nuptial re-lationship between Christ and the Church, although here again the problem of the Church as a subject on her own is presup-posed and alluded to, instead of being faced squarely and thought out.

It is difficult to assess, in this context, the import of the few *synoptic texts* which bridge the gap between the nuptial theology of the prophets and that of Paul. What stands out, here also, is their discretion, which goes so far that it is al-ways doubtful whether Jesus was describing himself as the bridegroom of the new redeemed community or was merely adopting the nuptial simile as the traditional image of the messianic era. In the parable of the ten virgins, there is probably no allusion to any bride;[1] the whole significance of the parable is the necessity of being always on the alert. The parable of the royal marriage feast (Mt. 22, 1–14) is about the judgment, and is obviously cognate with that of the wicked husbandmen (21, 33–46). Matthew puts them in close proximity. The passage about the "marriage guests" (Hebraistically called "sons of the bridegroom"), unable to mourn so long as the bridegroom is with them (Mt. 9, 15), cannot well be taken as a public declaration by Jesus of his messianic character. It is more like an application of a simile of Jesus by the community for its own acknowledgment of his being the Messiah. There remains only the word of the Baptist in St. John's Gospel (3, 29), that he who has the bride is the bridegroom, and the Baptist, the friend of the bridegroom, hears his voice and rejoices. This too can be reduced to a figure of speech, if we see in the Baptist the one who brings in the bride, he who, in the prevailing custom, had to bear witness to the bridegroom of the bride's virginity. Accordingly, the purport of the statement would be the friend's unselfish love. Such a minimizing of the text, however, is not obligatory; and it is far more probable that the Lord, of set purpose, took the marriage-image for the messianic era, and applied it to himself. This means no more than that he took it in the received Old Testament sense, according to which the bride is none other than the people as a collective entity, the community elected by the Lord.

We are still, in fact, a long way from the Pauline parallel of the physical relationship between man and wife, since the Lord himself, in his various utterances, does not anticipate what the creative "word of the cross" (1 Cor. 1, 18) would later express. And though, in the synoptics, the bridegroom is spoken of in quite clear fashion, it is remarkable that there is no mention of the bride, even in the parable of the royal marriage feast. It is left completely open who the bride is: whether the

1. The reading "to meet the bridegroom" seems the original one; "and the bride," a later addition (Mt. 25, 1).

bridegroom, in fact, has an individual bride, of whom the invited guests are friends or relations, or whether the nature of the bride is to be looked for as present, in a hidden manner, in the guests, the "children of the bridegroom," the ten virgins, and so in those very persons to whom the Lord is speaking. Again, the words of the Baptist, in St. John, taken by themselves, do not point to anything beyond the messianic connection; they do so only if taken as part of the general content and significance of the Gospel, along with the Word being made flesh (1, 14), the marriage feast at Cana (2, 1–11), the "temple of his body" (2, 21), the return to the womb in order to be reborn (3, 4), the giving of his flesh and blood for the life of the world (6, 33 f.), the fountain of living water flowing from him (7, 37–38), his freely giving his life for the sheep (10, 17), the royal entry of the "daughter of Zion" (12, 15), the vine and its branches (15, 1–8), his giving his mother to the disciple (19, 27), the opening of his side (19, 34), the breathing of the Holy Spirit (20, 22), the hand in the wound (20, 27)—and, the outcome of all this, the designation of the Church as "the elect lady and her children" (2 Jn. 1), and the eschatological vision of the spouse of the Lamb (Rev. 21, 22).

If we consider all these together, there is no doubt that, for St. John in particular, the relation between Christ and the Church goes far beyond that between Yahweh and Israel. A far more intimate relationship has been created and communicated through Christ's bodily nature, one transcending even that conveyed in the nuptial image of the Letter to the Ephesians, though including it. It is an intimacy more implied than expressed, and yet, in spite of it, St. John is as silent as the other evangelists on the personal character of the bride-Church. Even in the final eschatological vision of Revelation, he shows it only as in an image. He describes her appearance, adornment, splendor radiating outwards, just as does the Deutero-Isaiah, but never goes so far as to personify her. He ascribes to her no personal act, never exhorts her to rejoice, to marvel at the

multitude of her children. In fact, he lets her personality merge
with her social aspect, describing her as a city with a high wall
around her and twelve towers, dwelling on their position and
names, and describing in detail the interior arrangements, light-
ing, occupants, water supply, and structure. Only at the end of
the book and of the whole of Scripture do we hear a word from
the bride, her only word, uttered in unison with the Spirit: a
cry of longing to the bridegroom: "Come!" (22, 17).

Throughout, John is always more reserved than the prophets,
who ascribe a much more varied personal activity to the faithful
virgin and faithless prostitute, Zion. Though he presupposes a
far closer union as an existing fact, he restricts the personal
confrontation of bridegroom and bride to a minimum, and
even the bride's cry at the end can very well be interpreted in
the context of the collective idea. With this accords the fact
that John, who has nothing about the simile of Head and body,
carries on the two other great old covenant symbols of the
Church, that of the "vineyard" (Is. 5; 1 f.; Jer. 2, 21 f.), and
that of the "shepherd and the flock" (Jer. 23, 3 f.; Ez. 34). The
first he uses as an image of the community of being between
Jesus and the faithful, the second as an image of the Church's
collective unity reinstated by the shepherd.

If we go on to examine the theology of the Fathers, we find
it difficult not to speak of an extension and amplification of the
bride-motive that is not certainly authorized by Scripture: the
Church (even though come forth from Christ, or purified and
exalted by him) is made a subject on its own, with a womanly
beauty, whose form and adornment, feelings and sentiments,
destinies, humiliations, and exaltations can be described. A
powerful contribution to endowing the Church with a personality and life of its own was made, from the earliest times
(of Justin and Irenaeus), by the parallel drawn between Mary
and the Church, which, in the twelfth century, came to pervade
the commentaries on the Song: the Church as bride, difficult to
grasp in herself as a person, appears as it were polarized in the
person of Mary, and Mary herself as crystallizing around her-

self the whole community of the faithful. This idea may well have been, up to the present, the most suggestive for a personal conception of the Church. It is certainly the only one that, theologically, retains its force and is taken seriously. But, as with the older ecclesiological motives, the question must be asked: What is the theological justification for this extension? Has it any scriptural basis? Is it viable for us today? These questions cannot be evaded.

The contemporary doctrine of the Church goes further than an ecclesiology of the hierarchic and sacramental structure which communicates the grace of Christ; it is focused primarily on the simile of the body. Two phases may be distinguished of what is, in fact, a reaction against the official Counter-Reformation theology: the first is that of the organic conception of Catholic romanticism, and the second, in the present century, that of a renewed attention to the ideas of St. Paul, culminating in the encyclical *Mystici Corporis* and the theologies preceding and following it. The basic fact to be realized is that the Church is something more than a "structure" set up by Christ, an institution designed to shelter and sustain a multitude of believers in Christ, as a formal element enlcosing a material one. It is something that, in a mysterious way, is connected with the corporeal nature, the humanity, of Christ, preluded by his incarnation, prepared by his preaching, and finally established by his death on the cross and, above all, by the Eucharist as the fruit of the passion: a mystical participation in his hypostatic union, his person subsisting in two natures. What this change has above all restored to prominence is that the body of Christ in its three forms (*corpus triforme*), the real, the ecclesial (mystical), and the Eucharistic body, can be one and the same, inasmuch as the Eucharistic body is truly and actually the real body, but in a way that permits it to incorporate those who receive it as a mystical body.

This mysterious relationship, which can never be fully elucidated, goes far beyond the plane of the visible structure of the Church, or rather shows its true significance and its whole scope.

The mystery, however, as a Eucharistic one, is involved in this structure and given over to its charge; it is only accessible to the individual believer in the framework of the hierarchical structure. In this way, the doctrine of the *corpus mysticum* reacts powerfully on the conception of the hierarchical Church, giving it an added strength, and depth of meaning: the sacrament is "confected" by the priest, and through the power of his orders the laity participate in it. And what is true of the Eucharist is basically true of the other sacraments (with certain exceptions, to which we shall return). It is equally true of the Church's external and internal jurisdiction, which imprints the real ecclesiological form on the life of the Christian even in his inmost acts.

To such an image of the Church, in which the institutional and the Eucharistic-sacramental elements are so bonded, the matrimonial simile is almost an embarrassment. For if the two elements together illuminate the reality set up by Christ, signifying his spiritual achievement as well as his manhood, passion, and resurrection, nevertheless it only *formally* illuminates *that* reality which awaits the faithful, the "structure" which fulfills and completes them materially. The sacramental structure and the grace it contains is the aspect of the Church which proceeds directly from Christ, and it pertains only to those who are able to constitute a complementary reality. But it is difficult to see how this formal element, taken by itself, can be the basis, even figuratively, for a mutual personal relationship. Certainly, no one would want to say that this formal aspect, this form-giving (and *esse sequitur formam*) structure, taken by itself, is the Church; for the latter requires its material complement, the faithful themselves, who only become the people of God when "informed" by the Church-structure, and only represent the full reality of the bride of Christ within this structure. At the same time, it remains true that the faithful, both individually and as members of the community, can pertain to the Church as bride only insofar as they come within this form. They belong by grace of this form; they belong insofar as their lives are in

125

harmony with this form, and allow it to exist in them and work in them; for this form contains and imparts to them the grace of Christ and the Trinity, which makes them living members of the mystical body. But if the Church, as institution and sacrament, cannot be designated in the proper sense as bride of Christ, then the Church fully constituted (of form and matter) can rightly bear the personal name of bride only insofar as the people of the Church, coming under this form, receives it into itself and lets it work there—as a community, in other words.

This, much abbreviated, is roughly the line adopted by Charles Journet in his work *The Church of the Word Incarnate,* the fullest treatise in ecclesiology in our time. He is fond of citing the dictum of St. Thomas that Christ, Head and body, *"computatur quasi una persona,"* [1] for everything that formally constitutes the Church and whereby she draws men to Christ is physically and morally an outflowing of Christ, who represents the *"personalité mystique efficiente instrumentale"* of the Church. Moreover, Journet says, "since Christ as man is king, priest, and saviour, it is in the likeness of his kingdom, his priesthood, and his charity that he sets his stamp on the Church, making henceforth with her but a single living being, a single mystical person inundated with grace from on high. Of this mystical person he constitutes himself, by his sacred humanity, the mystical personality effecting it but only instrumentally," since the ultimate agent is the Trinity itself, or, *per appropriationem,* the Holy Spirit. As the source from which the prayer of intercession ascends, Christ and the Church in conjunction form a single mystical person. Likewise, such a person is formed by the Holy Spirit and the Church together as the source from which grace descends and works its effects. "The Church's life is, indeed, inseparable from its source, from the Word of God in the order of intercessory prayer, from the Holy Spirit in the order of action. Yet the Church can be contemplated also for itself, in abstraction from its source from which it is distin-

1. *Summa Theol.,* III, 49, 1.

guished. . . . Here is the place for the bridal comparison. The Church then appears as a created collective person, distinct from Christ as bride from bridegroom, and from the Spirit as creature from Creator." But it is clear from the whole context that such an abstraction is wholly artificial, since the underlying distinction between "uncreated" grace (the presence of the divine Spirit) and "created" grace (as the *direct* effect of this presence) in the preceding case does not essentially elucidate anything, since the created grace itself cannot for a moment be thought of apart from the uncreated. One cannot even say that the formal element here under consideration is already described in the Bible as "body of Christ," since this necessarily includes in its definition the concrete members as the material element. Still less is the formal element to be designated the "bride."

Consequently, we are obliged to affirm that, if there is to be a nuptial (and so some kind of personal) contradistinction between Christ and the Church—however this may subsequently be determined—the basis of it lies, indeed, in God's life imparted but no less essentially in the subjectivity and personality of the real subjects who form the Church.

3. PETER AND MARY

Let us accept this view, without prematurely drawing the conclusion that, in so doing, we fall back on a purely collectivistic conception. What it excludes is simply the naïve, unreflecting hypostasizing of the "bride," although ultimately such a hypostasizing, once fully clarified by reflexion, will be perfectly acceptable as an adequate expression of the mystery. It excludes, in addition, the view prevailing in the late Middle Ages and the Counter-Reformation as a consequence of a weakening of the earlier insight; the view, that is, that the hierarchical and sacramental structure of the Church is the Church in the strict or formal sense, while the "sheep" ruled by the hierarchy and merely receptive of the sacraments belong only to the "material" element of the Church. On the contrary, the whole structural aspect of the Church is also mediating and instrumental, and even the various modes of divine communication in the Christological graces of the Church are not an end in themselves, but are for the sake of those who receive them. The whole purpose of the formal structure and sacramental grace is to reach out to the human person as he actually is, to penetrate his being and raise him to the status of member of the mystical Head: only thus is "the Church" constituted.

The encounter which, at its maximum intensity, merits the name of marriage is personal and takes place between God as person and man as person; though all that gives this encounter an ecclesiological stamp is its prerequisite only, and is not the encounter itself. Admittedly, the whole complex of those things instituted by God for salvation is the most sublime, the richest in mystery, the most inaccessible to the human mind, of all that is. Nonetheless, it is there for the sake of the individual creature, and only fulfills its purpose when he is reached and brought home to God. Much in these institutions is, in the deepest sense, conditioned by time, and disappears when fulfillment is reached in the next world. That is the case with the official, hierarchic structure of the Church and its individual sacraments, and also with certain provisional forms of the life of grace they impart: faith and love in their veiled condition, the cardinal virtues as conditioned by time and the necessity of struggle. What never falls away is the nuptial encounter between God and the creature, for whose sake the framework of the structures is now set up and will later be dismantled. This encounter, therefore, must be the real core of the Church. The structures and the graces they impart are what raise up the created subjects to what they should be in God's design; a humanity formed as a bride to the Son, become the Church.

The bride is essentially woman, that is, receptive; one who, through acceptance of the seed, but also through all her own female organs and powers, is made competent to bring forth and bear fruit. In bringing forth at birth (which, in a broad sense, includes her care of the child and his feeding and upbringing to full independence), woman gives to man the complete, superabundant response. It is to such a Christian womanly role that the creature is educated by the structural, sacramental Church: the office and the sacrament are forms of communicating the seed; they belong to the male aspect, but their end is to lead the bride to her womanly function and fortify her in it. Part of this, indeed, is her ability to receive a supernatural seed, an ability which itself is capable of development from a low to a high potential; and it includes, besides, the power to preserve the seed, to make it bring forth much fruit in the "good ground," a hundred-, sixty-, and thirtyfold (Mt. 15, 8–9). In the supernatural sphere of the Church one cannot assume an encounter, on equal terms, between two partners for the imparting of the seed, as one can in the natural order. Here, on the contrary, the preparation of the female partner is, fundamentally, conjoined with the nuptial act of union, and both together are meant by St. Paul with the active verb "to present" (Eph. 5, 27). Considered in the terms of Church law, it is true that the representative of the "office" has the masculine function of the one who gives, and the "laity" the feminine one of receiving; but it does not follow that the clergy are "more," the laity "less," the Church. The reverse is, in fact, the case, since the active communication is instrumental, the passive reception is the end, essentially ordered, to indeed basically one with, the female activity of seed-bearing, giving birth, and educating.

Admittedly, this distinction between means and end is not of itself sufficient to make clear the genesis of the Church as a subject in her own right, since the structures by which grace is mediated do not exist apart in a sort of space between Christ and the Church; they belong to the latter. In this connection, it is pertinent to take note of the fact that Christ also did not establish them in a void, but in the growing faith of his disciples, a faith already come to maturity in Peter's confession. "Lord, to whom shall we go? You have the words of eternal life; and we have believed, and have come to know, that you are the Holy One of God" (Jn. 6, 68–69). This is a faith that knows and is able to express what it knows, a knowledge it owes, not to "flesh and blood," but to "the Father who draws," the Father to whom faith makes men tractable and docile (Jn. 6, 44–45). The Church's faith is the womb which can bring to birth, to assist which the Church's functions were framed. This makes the foundation, in the gifts it brings, strictly parallel to the demand of following Christ even to the death of the cross, likewise a gift of grace given and assured (Jn. 21, 18–19). The functions belong to the Church bearing and giving birth; her womb is where they are preserved; there they were received, and from there are imparted.

This alone explains why, for the Fathers, it was precisely in her sacramental action that the Church appeared as a mother's womb giving birth, and as a mother bringing up those born to her. "The Church lies in anguish," St. Methodius says, "and bears the *psychike* anew as *pneumatike;* for this reason, she is also a mother. For as the woman receives the man's yet unformed seed, and, in the course of time, brings a complete man to the world, so, we may say, the Church continually receives those who betake themselves to the *Logos,* shapes them into the image and form of Christ, and makes them, in the course of time, citizens of those blessed eternities. . . . Those whom she gives birth to, are the neophytes, . . . and these receive the characteristics, the human mode of Christ, because the image and form of the *Logos* is impressed on them, and born in them through perfect gnosis and pistis, so that in them Christ is born in a spiritual manner. And, therefore, the Church is pregnant and in travail, till Christ is formed and born in us, in order that each one of the saints may be born as Christ through his participation in Christ." Here the antithesis between office as directed to an end and reception as the end envisaged is resolved in a higher identity, in that the womb of the Church effects prototypically in the individual what the individual himself will have to bring about through his being patterned in this womb. This again supposes that the Church as prototype, if she is to be able to perform the sacramental function, her-

self possesses not only the "objective holiness" of the structures, but the subjective, personal holiness of faith, love, and
hope realised in act. Therein she is already, in the fullest sense,
the bride who can make to the bridegroom and his "word of
the cross" (1 Cor. 1, 18) the creaturely, bridal response expected of her—creaturely, because her love is believing and
hoping, not seeing and possessing; bridal, because her loving
faith and hope is formed supernaturally by Christ's "word of
the cross."

All of this can be expressed in a different way: if the content of the ecclesiastical structure is, for the Church herself,
"objective spirit," whose scope and range can only be measured and grasped by the divine subjectivity (for God alone
completely "understands" his own Word, which the disciples
proclaim; God alone fully perceives the greatness of the grace
which they mediate sacramentally; and God alone knows the
divine severity inherent from its foundation in the Church's
jurisdiction, when it is applied according to the mind of God),
then this "objective spirit" necessarily presupposes a "subjective spirit" to receive it. This is Peter's faith. It is obvious,
however, that it does not inhere absolutely and exclusively in
the subject, Peter. Its existence is only witnessed and represented by Peter at the promise of the office (Mt. 16) and its
bestowal (Jn. 21), as is abundantly clear by the Lord's threefold question before the investiture. What this act brings out
above all is that Peter's subjective spirit is not equal to the
objective spirit of office and sacrament, not only because Peter
is a sinner and his sinfulness was never more terribly revealed
than when he was confronted with the demands inherent in
the spirit of the office, but even more so because Christ alone
can bring unison into the two sides in the uniqueness and
singularity of his mission as redeemer and mediator. There is
one only who can be both priest and sacrifice, one only who
can bring together in unison the divine demands of worship
and expiation inherent in the priestly office. The identity to
which the office points cannot, by any means, exist in the

131

Church, but solely in the Lord, as the Church's Head and Bridegroom.

Yet, and just because of this, this identity must be reproduced in the Church; for the Lord wills to see his Church standing before him, not as a singular, palpable failure, but as a glorious bride worthy of him. Here the Marian principle in the Church necessarily comes into play. Mary is the subjectivity which, in its womanly and receptive manner, is enabled fully to correspond to the masculine subjectivity of Christ, through God's grace and the overshadowing of his Spirit. The Church flowing forth from Christ finds her personal center in Mary as well as the full realization of her idea as Church. Her faith, with its love and hope, in its womanly openness to the divine, the divine-human Bridegroom, is co-extensive with the masculine principle, embedded in the Church, of office and sacrament, even though it is not part of its womanly character to comprehend totally, in the manner of the bridegroom, the objective spirit therein contained. She is not the Word, but the adequate response awaited by God from the created sphere, and produced in it by his grace through the Word.

For this, undoubtedly, a special grace is needed, qualitatively different from that of the rest of the faithful, which elevates the Marian response of faith to the status of principle and exemplar of the response of the entire Church. Mary's faith, as the fruitful womb of the Word, is privileged on two counts. In respect of its origin, it is a faith proceeded from her "immaculate conception"; in respect of its end, it is a faith destined to bear the fruit which is not only Christ's body, but himself as Head. This fruitfulness, therefore, which was previously predicated of the Church as prototype of the fruitfulness of the members, when, from being born, passively, in baptism, they actively bring forth the life of Christ, in themselves and in the Church, —this paradigmatic fruitfulness is, in Mary, so far surpassed, raised to such potency, that she not only does what the Church does—bring forth Christ—but does it archetypally, in that she lets the Head of the Church take flesh in her, him whom the Church will, in turn, deliver from out of herself. The process on the ecclesial level, whereby the soul born of Christ in turn conceives and bears him, in the order of the body, this process is elevated to become an archetypal process in which Mary, preserved from original sin by the grace of Christ's cross, conceives and bears him in the order of the Head. In the former process, the objective stainlessness of the Church (the "infallibility of Peter") always effects and supposes a constant purification of the Church by water and the Word, and, therefore, the Church becomes a "glorious bride" only as she is actually made pure. But in the process on the Marian level there can be no question of a subjective, personal purification as an actual event. Mary, preserved from the outset, has undergone no such purification. In Mary, therefore, the Church is not only infallible in the official sacrament sphere (though always fallible subjectively and existentially, always defective and hopelessly falling short of the ideal inherent and proclaimed). In her the Church is also personally immaculate, and beyond the tension between reality and ideal.

It is on this very account that Mary also stands above and beyond the purely mundane encounter of bridegroom and bride, and opens it out into the infinity of the divine Eros insofar as God himself accepts her word of faith and fidelity, and as she is overshadowed, not by the *Logos* as such, but by the Holy Spirit, who carries the Father's seed into her spiritual and bodily womb, the fruit of this marriage being the incarnation of the Son, who, in his entire being, is head and body, bridegroom and bride. There is certainly no question of making a personal distinction, in the union of husband and wife, between the man giving and the seed given, and from this standpoint Mary, as prototype of the Church, is rightly called the bride of the incarnate Word. Nonetheless, what is brought about here is not a repetition of the sex-relationship, but its prototypal realization between God and man; and God, known and received in this intimate fashion, can only be the God in three Persons. On this account, Mary receives the Son as seed of the Father through

133

the realizing act of the Holy Spirit of Father and Son. And it is for the same reason that, in the sphere of the Church, the actualizing of the sacraments is the work of the Holy Spirit, who places the Father's Word in the womb of the soul for it to generate and give birth. This again does not prevent the Church being the Son's bride, since this entire participation of the created world in the Trinitarian divinity is the working and prolongation of the Incarnate Word. Mary is given to us as prototype so that the Church may never forget the Trinitarian dimension of her nuptial mystery; just as Christ, too, as he went about on earth, always situated it in relation to an openness to the Trinitarian life.

There is another thing that this reveals, namely, the reason why, according to St. Thomas, the *fiat* of the mother of God was spoken *loco totius generis humani* and not, for instance, *loco totius Ecclesiae*. (It could equally be said that, in her, the Church speaks her *fiat* to God for the whole human race.) The Word was, in fact, carried into her life of faith in a womb, in order to become flesh. It is part of her mystery and being that the Word became flesh, not only in her, but from her, that her self-giving response to God was understood and required as something involving the whole person, something both spiritual and of the body. One cannot divide this response into two parts: one spiritual, her active acceptance of faith; the other bodily, her passive utilization as womb for God becoming man. It is for this very reason that she participated in the formation of the hypostatic union in her own manner, a purely womanly one of surrender. And when the Fathers see the actual *connubium* between God and man realized in Christ himself, in the indissoluble union of the two natures, this is also no purely physical occurrence, with its matrimonial character exclusively derived from the side of God and his intention. It is a real two-sided mystery of love through the bridal consent of Mary acting for all the rest of created flesh. In Mary's flesh is meant "all" created "flesh" (Jn. 17, 2) to which God wills to espouse himself; and since Mary is *caro ex qua*, she is also *fides ex qua*. But the hypostatic union is the carrying out, and thus the final indissoluble sealing of the covenant of fidelity, which marks with its sign all future vows of fidelity in the Church: those of baptism, of marriage, and of virginity.

Mary's abiding physical virginity is the bodily aspect of the abiding inner virginity, which means the exclusiveness, of her spiritual faith. The glorification of virginity by the Fathers, which they apply both to the Church's virginity and to that of those vowed to it and of each individual member of the Church, even the married, is directed, fundamentally, to a Marian virginity, itself primarily the expression of a personal attitude to the God coming to meet them nuptially. Once again, we can follow out two themes in this glorification: the Church, from her very origin, is virginal (as distinct from the synagogue, so often reproached by God as an adulteress). Also, the Church, as the one "purified" by Christ, has become "virginal," and as she is constantly protected by this grace, she must keep herself in the virginity received and not fall away from it again. But both Mary and the Church are fruitful precisely because they are virginal. The exclusive character of love, which virginity involves, is in each the condition for bearing the fruit of God. The themes interlace in the happiest way when the two acts— the "purification" of the Church, and her divine marriage—are seen as one, as in the celebrated Benedictus-antiphon of the Epiphany.

Dom Odo Casel has brought out the idea (originally Syrian and subsequently adopted in the West) that the Epiphany is the feast of the marriage between Christ and the Church in that the baptismal water of the Jordan was also understood as the fructifying water of the marriage: "In the river Jordan has the Church become espoused," sings the Syrian Church during matins of the vigil. The bath of the bridegroom is, at the same time, the marriage bath of the bride, since the bride herself is present prototypically in the flesh of the bridegroom. For this reason, the Epiphany can be, in the East, both the baptismal day of all believers and the day of the consecration of virgins; for

135

the sacramental bath is itself the enactment of the nuptial mystery, and the consecration of virgins is done to exemplify the marriage between Christ and the Church, being the explicitation of what had been begun in the baptismal vows and fulfilled in the conferring of the sacrament. What essentially demonstrates this for us is that the sacramental baptism received by the individual Christian was originally received by the Church herself, and indeed in the flesh of Christ, which, nuptially united to his Godhead, is the source of the "mystical body."

The outcome of our study so far is that the first step to answering, in a positive way, the question as to the subject of the Church is to relate it to Mary's faith, fruitful because virginal. Alois Müller has rightly shown that the patristic parallel between Mary and the Church, though it contains all the elements for the solution, failed of final elucidation because it was never made sufficiently clear that Mary's faith was what made possible her bodily conception of Christ, and so there was no advance beyond a mere parallel between her bodily bringing forth and the Church's spiritual bringing forth. But once all doubt on the point was overcome, the act of Mary was seen, absolutely, as the basic subjective act of the Church. For Mary's personal act, by reason of its uniqueness and eminence, can be two things at once: the subjective and absolutely complete ground for the subjective act of the Church as such (always qualitatively superior to every act, defective as it is, of the individual); and, since Mary is also an individual believer within the Church community, the subjective and absolutely complete ground of each personal act of faith within the *communio sanctorum*. At the same time, it must always be borne in mind that, as we said before, the subjective act of the Church, even in its perfect fullness in that of Mary, is always one of womanly surrender—an act, not of dominance and comprehension (which pertains to the Head), but of humble, handmaidenly following and service. Its character is not one of masculine gnosis, desire for knowledge at all costs; for Mary on earth did not seek after knowledge, but was content to keep and contemplate the word in her heart. Even the theological and pastoral knowledge and understanding that the risen Christ laid up in the memory of his Church in opening, for forty days, the Scripture to his apostles, was placed deep within this spiritual womb of womanly contemplation. And so, in this respect also, the prophecy was fortified: *femina circumdabit virum.*

Mary, in giving birth spiritually and physically to the Son, becomes the universal mother of all believers, for the Church as body is born of Christ and is herself Christ. Mary is the prototype of the Church, not only because of her virginal faith, but equally because of her fruitfulness. This is, indeed, not autonomous (as that of the goddesses of fertility), but wholly ancillary, since it is Christ, not Mary, who brought the Church into being by his passion. All the same, she took part, as an intermediary, in this creation by the universality and unrestrictedness of her *fiat,* which the Son is able to use as an infinitely plastic medium to bring forth from it new believers, those born again. Her presence with him at the cross, her agreement to his abandonment of her to the Church in the midst of his dereliction on the cross, her eternal role as the woman in labor (Rev. 12), show how fully her self-surrender is universalized to become the common source, the productive womb, of all Christian grace.

4. ANIMA ECCLESIASTICA

Mary's special role as regards the new people of God in the history of salvation gives part of the answer to the question "Who is the Church?" It cannot give the whole answer, but what it can do is usher in the complete answer, since it is the infinite disponibility of her attitude of faith ("be it done unto me according to thy word") that makes her the ideal (moral) and real (physical) womb of the Church. Her own person, in its faith, love, and hope, has become so supple in the hand of the Creator that he can extend her beyond the limits of a private consciousness to a Church consciousness, to what the older theology since Origen and Ambrose is accustomed to call *anima ecclesiastica.*

This *"ecclesiasticizing" of the individual consciousness* is, however, available on a different level to every man regenerated from the private existence of the natural state and the still more cramped bounds of sin-consciousness estranged from God, regenerated, that is, to the Church through the death of the old man, and endowed with the consciousness of the new man. The truths propounded here are such as the "old man" cannot grasp, eluding the subtlest philosophical dialectic of alternation with its progressive broadening out of consciousness into the Absolute. The fact is that the dying and burial of the old man has already taken place *"en Christô,"* and so likewise the resurrection of the new, who lives *"en Christô,"* ontologically, and so, of necessity, also consciously. "Therefore if any one is in Christ, he is a new creation; the old has passed away, behold, the new has come" (2 Cor. 5, 17).

The newness in question consists not in a diminution, still less in an extinction of personal consciousness, but in its being taken along in faith into the consciousness of Christ: "it is no longer I who live, but Christ who lives in me; and the life I now live in the flesh I live by faith in the Son of God, who loved me and gave himself for me" (Gal. 2, 20). "And he died for all, that those who live might live no longer for themselves but for him who for their sake died and was raised" (2 Cor. 5, 15). "If we live, we live to the Lord, and if we die, we die to the Lord; so then, whether we live or whether we die, we are the Lord's" (Rom. 14, 8). This constantly renewed and variously expressed expropriation of man, in which he dies to himself, is, in its positive aspect, his appropriation by God, to "obtain salvation" (1 Thess. 5, 9). The expression is never used in a singular sense, however: it always refers to God's own people" (1 Pet. 2, 9), and only as such are they called to "obtain the glory of our Lord Jesus Christ" (2 Thess. 2, 13). This taking up of the "I" and the "we" through God into Christ is often described by Paul as a changeover from consciousness of one's own action to consciousness of God's action taking place within us: "Not that I have already obtained this or am already perfect; but I press on to make it my own, because Christ Jesus has made me his own" (Phil. 3, 12). "But if one loves God, one is known by him" (1 Cor. 8, 3). ". . . what we are is known to God" (2 Cor. 5, 11). ". . . you have come to know God, or rather to be known by God" (Gal. 4, 9). And, eschatologically: "Now I know in part; then I shall understand fully, even as I have [now already] been fully understood" (1 Cor. 13, 12).

What kind of consciousness this is of the new man, according to Paul (and also, of course, John, Peter, and James), comes out most clearly from his use of the personal pronouns. Paul makes copious use of the first person singular. His "I" has astonishing vitality, diversity, agility: in fact, with regard to the community, it has a kind of omnipresence beyond space and time—*absens corpore, praesens spiritu* (absent in body . . . present in spirit"—1 Cor. 5, 3). He uses "I" in speaking of such a commonplace thing as the plan of a journey which he propounds, but also in speaking of the vertiginous height of his solitary calling in God's plan of salvation: ". . . you have heard of the stewardship of God's grace that was given to me for you, how the mystery was made known to me by revelation, as I have written briefly. When you read this you can perceive my insight into the mystery of Christ" (Eph. 3, 2–4). His "I" is of such unique character, is so patterned on Christ and imitative of him as to be recommended, in its turn, for imitation. It had its beginning at Damascus. It is the "I" of Christ's mission, the "I" transformed into the servant of Christ, from flesh become spirit. It is ecclesiastical, and manifests itself—brings out its own anatomy before the eyes of all—only because it is a paradigm of the mission, the functional side of the Church, of membership in the body of Christ. It knows itself as utterly divested of ownership of itself; belonging wholly to Christ and the communion of saints, it would prefer to die so as to be with Christ, that being by far the best—but it no longer knows any personal preference: what is best for Paul is what serves the Church best, and for her sake he continues to live (Phil. 1, 23–25).

We can see from this that to attempt to write a psychology of Paul is no less absurd, in principle, than to do the same of Christ. The personal reality that drives forward with such impetus cannot, by its very nature, be contained in these categories, although it does not destroy them (which is what tantalizes the onlooker so much), but makes sovereign use of them. It is because the "I" of Christ harbors the Father and the Spirit in circumincession that he can release out of himself the mystical body with all his personal members, their missions of sanctification and functions of love. And because the Trinitarian "I" of Christ wills to dwell in those who love him (Jn. 14, 23), the "I" of Paul is not only entirely dominated by this divine life, but harbors, for its part, the communities entrusted to him, which he brings forth in travail out of himself (Gal. 4, 19), and to which he is father, mother, and nurse. His "anxiety for all the Churches" (2 Cor. 11, 28) is a womanly weakness, accepted in order to produce manly strength, a weakness that, together with Christ, is the ignominy of the cross and a spectacle to men and angels. Yet even on this plane the law holds good: "... children ought not to lay up for the parents, but parents for their children. I will most gladly spend and be spent for your souls" (2 Cor. 12, 14–15). He justifies even his severity as an educator by this love, and lets his tenderness shine through all his harsh measures. And he so utterly experiences the glory of Christ pervading him that he has no call whatever to glorify himself, but is wholly and entirely the glory of the churches.

This "I"—explicable in terms of the mission, and not of psychology—, which the Church bears in herself, and which has expanded to become the *anima ecclesiastica,* is now able to think and to say things about the Church, quite beyond the reach of a personal "I." This occurs when, in the course of its official function, it has to contrast itself with the "you" of those in its charge and can, therefore, include with its own content the content of the churches and communities—and so, also, the content of the "you." In such cases, it can use the ecclesiastical "we" in statements bearing on salvation, which none of the individuals addressed could presume to do. Take the beginning of the Letter to the Ephesians, where the Father's eternal plan of salvation is described from predestination onwards, and where the "we" designates the Church of the predestined. In this "we," Paul himself is, of course, included. His assurance of salvation is as absolute as that of the Church herself (which prevents neither him nor the actual Church from supporting this assurance by fervent prayer and penance—"lest, while I preach to others, I myself become a castaway"). But he absolutely includes within it the community of which he has actual charge, not in a vague, rhetorical "we," but in the "we" of the father, of the responsible apostle, who gathers his children around him as a hen gathers her brood under her wings (Mt. 23, 38); yet the parrhesia for doing so he derives from his mission and office. It is only when admonishing and censuring in his function as educator, that he opposes himself to the community, or, at any rate, excludes himself from it *ad tempus;* while in his preaching office he includes himself, and his consciousness of the Church can compensate for any lack of parrhesia in the utterance of others. ". . . become as I am, for I also have become as you are" (Gal. 4, 12). That is, you too must allow yourselves to be formed by the Church: "And we exhort you, brethren, admonish the idle, encourage the faint-hearted, help the weak, be patient with them all. See that none of you repays evil for evil, but always seek to do good to one another and to all" (1 Thess. 5, 14–15). It is clear from this that the "Church of the saints" not only "represents" the Church of sinners, of the imperfect, the struggling, but also carries them and is responsible for them before God. With Christ it empties itself, so as, in weakness and shame, to bring in the least member, and to be able to represent each such, not only in word, in reprimanding, but in deed and in truth.

Thus the opposition between "I" and "you" ("Thou") is always reconciled by the "we" which joins them together, and the transition from one to the other is smooth and imperceptible.

"We" can mean: (1) the person of Paul in his office. The plural, then, expresses the neutralization of the person by his office, but, at the same time, emphasizes the function, which, as such, is always represented by a plurality of subjects. The transition from this "official" to the "theological" (carrying and including) plural remains imperceptible (see 1 Thess. 3, 1. 3–4. 6 f., where, in verse 5, the "I" suddenly emerges from the "we"); (2) the hierarchs, for instance Paul with Timothy and Silvanus as joint authors of the letter, where Paul either purposely includes the others or, forgetting them for the moment and speaking from the fullness of his own heart, includes them only implicitly. The "party of the hierarchs" can also pass over, without a break, into the "party of the Church," since the teachers have confidence in it manifesting what is taught in its mode of life; (3) or this account, "we" can simply mean the Christians in the Church, Paul and the community together.

"You" is either (1) the individual community spoken to, or (2) a considerable section of the Church, for instance the Gentile Christians, to whom Paul speaks as a Jew from the other side, or alternatively, the Jewish Christians, whom Paul appeals to as the apostle of the Gentiles. But it can also be (3) simply "you Christians," you baptized, dead and risen in Christ; and then its scope is coincident with the "we" in the last signification. In this case, it is indifferent whether Paul uses "you" or "we": he is carrying on the inner colloquy of the Church with herself; he gives utterance to her self-consciousness, either as he is authorized to do so, or (which comes to the same thing) as the voice of the whole. This applies equally to questions of fact and of obligation. Consequently, it does not matter if the instruction proceeds from the "we" to the "you" (1 Thess. 4, 1 f.), and then again comprises both in a common "we" (4, 14), continuing in the "you" only again to include the "you" in the "we," and to establish a rigid exclusion from those not belonging to the Church and from their conduct (5, 5–10). In Galatians 6, 1–10, "I" alternates with "you," "thou," and "we"; all facets of the Church-consciousness that never impairs the person, but protects and elevates it to a superior order.

This analysis shows that the birth of the new man, belonging specifically to the Church in the grace of baptism, in the outpouring of faith, hope, and love through the Holy Spirit (Rom. 5, 1–5), means the extension of the narrow limits of the individual sinful subject as compared with the subject of the Church. This does not imply that the believer becomes Christ substantially, nor does it mean a direct participation in the hypostatic union; nor, indeed, a progressive pantheism according to Eckhart, or as Hegel teaches in such an extreme sense. On the other hand, the mysteries of the *communio sanctorum,* the degree of the mutual circumincession of the members, their mutual power of representation before God, their community of goods even of the most inward, the monadic power to love to draw everything on itself and into itself (as described in particular by Tauler), and, as a result, to extend itself over everything and, while remaining a single heart, to become one *cor mundi:* these mysteries cannot be adequately mastered by means of purely philosophical distinctions (*"entitative* singular, *intentionaliter* universal"). The theological paradoxes are sharper; and it is simply a question of preserving their sharpness and not reducing one side to the other. They are paradoxes that thrust themselves on our attention from the indwelling of the Trinity in the Church: for the Church is uniquely the sphere which binds God and creature together. Therefore, where the most improbable event must necessarily occur, —where, that is, the individual person, penetrated by God's dwelling in him—, is both elevated and sublimated in his personality and opened to and made the portion of the community. Here too the mysteries of the Trinitarian relations and of their opposition in identity cannot fail to impinge; and the mystery of Christ himself, who

143

in the Church is at once himself (his body) and another (his bride) works out in the Christian's life of grace in the Church. But with all this, the fundamental law of the creaturely status is not to be held superseded and overborne by the divine paradoxes to which man is raised. On the contrary, his elevation is what brings out clearly, confirms and fulfills the ultimate end of the created being as such (*gratia perficit naturam*). Looked at in this way, the laws of the *corpus mysticum* are commendable to reason, and that is why Paul could borrow his image of the body from the Romans. It is reasonable that the member should sacrifice itself for the *bonum commune,* as Cicero says, and after him Caiaphas (Jn. 11, 50), unconsciously prophesying, that is, not suspecting how truly he spoke. And it is equally in accord with any rational social order that the strong should care for the weak, and so bring about a balance (Rom. 15, 1 f.; 1 Cor. 8). But just how far this law can go is made manifest only in the Church.

5. UNITY IN ANALOGY

It follows that the Church is most fully present where faith, hope, and love, selflessness and tolerance of others, are found in the highest degree. Thus the concepts of "more" and "less" come into the Church, and the categories of proper and improper enter at the borderline where a living, loving, hoping faith passes, through mortal sin, into a "dead faith." These categories altogether dominate the ecclesiology of the Fathers. Later, when heretics definitely misapplied them, they were relegated to the background, making way for a univocal idea of the Church, but one tending of necessity to a certain minimalism. Still, in the long run, they remain indispensable for ecclesiology. They are dangerous only when they are warped, and so lead to inadmissible conclusions: for example, that the sinner, who possesses no more than a dead faith, can no longer be a member of the Church, or that the Church of the saints, and the official, institutional Church are magnitudes of different orders, of their nature disparate. We must keep two aspects simultaneously in mind, and hold them firmly: first, the Church is a unity—trinitarian, Christological, and plainly characterized as such in her own structure—; and, secondly, this unity is imprinted analogously on the members. Here it is not a question of the *analogia fidei*—the allocation of faith by God according to the quality of the mission of the members—, but of the categories of proper and improper, and, within the former, of the degrees of intensity within the participation.

The Fathers saw these two aspects expressed in the unity of the bride, the one single dove, and the plurality of her companions, those who follow in her train. *"Sponsa enim ipsa perfecta ecclesia est, sponsus Dominus, adulescentulae vero cum sponsa sunt inchoantes animae et per novum studium pubescentes"* (St. Gregory the Great). Origen had already given this interpretation, Origen, who was so fond of emphasizing the (fluid) analogy, in the Church, of the "simple" (or "progressive") and the "knowers" (or "perfect"). The "perfect" are those who have the *anima ecclesiastica,* having allowed their consciousness to merge with that of the Church, and so represent in themselves the essence of the one bride. One would have to blind oneself to the facts if one refused to admit that, for the Fathers and even for the high Middle Ages, the "proper" Church was that of those with living faith, those who love, and that, despite all the misapplications of this view by the Montanists, Novatians, Donatists, Messalianers, the extreme Origenists, and, later, the Bogomils and Catharists, despite all the Church's theological defences against these, the original, early Christian idea of an irrefragable partnership of Church and love, Church-unity and love-unity, lived on vigorously. Augustine himself, who had carried on in this field a bitter war against the "pure Church" of the Donatists and the sinlessness of the Pelagians, preferred to abandon the "unspottedness" of the present Church, 'and to make the "stainless bride" an eschatological reality, rather than to retreat from the idea of this partnership. Certainly, the Church is full of sinners, but *inas-*

145

much as they are sinners, they cannot be counted in with the Church. They can only be in her as "improper," "so-called," "seeming," "reckoned," "pretended" members, but cannot, *qua* sinners, express membership in the one body of love. It must be clearly noted that Augustine, in this, had no thought of splitting the Church into two (apparently irreconcilable) magnitudes: a Church of saints, the true one, and a Church of the external institution. He had no more idea of doing so than any of the other Fathers or the Scholastics.

Admittedly, Augustine's idea of the Church has within it a line of demarcation, derived from elsewhere, which has, indirectly, an ecclesiological consequence, and is not without a causal connection with the final cleavage in the Protestant idea of the Church. Let us look first at the relationship between the proper and the improper Church before Augustine. From the Gospel onwards, there is a "bearing" of the sinners in the Church; it is not without significance that, in John, Christ's answer to Peter's acknowledgment of the Messiah contains a reference to the presence of Judas among the twelve: "Did I not choose you, the twelve, and one of you is a devil?" (Jn. 6, 70). The line constantly taken by Paul in his ethical teaching is that Christians should bear with one another, that the more perfect (the "strong"), in particular, should endure the less perfect (the "weak"). The only kind of excommunication he uses is medicinal, leaving to God judgment on the question of definite membership. John, however (in the name of the Church), puts himself already in the situation of the final judgment, when he distinguishes between sins that are not unto (eternal) death, for which one can intercede, and those unto (eternal) death. "I do not say that one is to pray for that" (1 Jn. 5, 16). But can the line of demarcation between these two sins (not to be confused with our distinction between mortal and venial sins) ever be established in the temporal sphere? And as long as there remains a glimmer of hope for an apostate's conversion, surely the Church is obliged by the command to bear with and pray for him?

146

This command was taken absolutely by the pre-Augustinian Fathers as the rule of the Church. Origen describes the "perfect" or "gnostic" as the one who intercedes with God for the "imperfect," in fact, as the strong in Christ fighting the Pauline fight against the powers of darkness, on behalf of the weak. The "gnostic" or "knower" is, for Origen, precisely the "teacher," whether through theological instruction, if he is capable, or through the example of his life, preëminently through martyrdom. And so, out of Paul's teaching and his idea of the fruitfulness and convincing witness of holiness, we have the image of the Church wonderfully described, for example, by Methodius:

From the "rib" of the Son made man and lying dead on the cross (the rib being his spirit), God took the matter from which to form for him his "life partner." "I mean, of course, the souls betrothed and espoused to him; for it is the frequent usage of Scripture to call such the whole multitude of believers, and so the Church; and in this way the more perfect and advanced are brought together into the one person and the one body of the Church. The higher souls, who have a more inward grasp of the truth, cast away, in their perfect purity and perfect faith, the follies of the flesh, and thus become the life partners of Christ; to him they are, according to the words of the apostle, betrothed and espoused as a virgin, in order that they may receive within them the pure and fecund seed of doctrine, and coöperate as helpers in teaching for the redemption of others. But those who are still imperfect and only beginners in doctrine will be drawn by the more perfect into the pregnant womb of the redemption, and formed as in a mother's body, till they are born and brought to existence unto the greatness and beauty of virtue; for these, in turn, thanks, to their progress, have become the Church, and coöperate in the birth and training of other children, in that they accomplish the immaculate will of the Logos in the womb of their souls as in a mother's body."

This image of the Church constantly recurs throughout patristic theology. It is a dynamic image of love, a love striving up-

147

wards to the perfect, and, at the same time, descending with Christ to sustain and protect what is weak. This love, then, is not only a general well-wishing of children for one another, but one explicitly Christ-like in form, and only thus a Christian and ecclesial love, not stopping at the things "the heathens also do," but going on to what Christ has done and what each member after and along with the Head ought to do in the commission and power of Christ. Paul first demonstrated in himself this law of bearing the Church in its full application, and had, as it were, to experience in himself what is necessarily implied in the specific holiness of the Church. Therefore, the Fathers did not stretch the idea unduly in applying this active "bearing force" of Christian love to all who earnestly love Christ and the Church more than themselves, and become martyrs to her, whether or not by the shedding of their blood. This is what shows whether, in the consciousness of the individual, the Church outweighs the personal "I," and whether a "fellow runner" in the Church is a "bearer of the Church," a "pillar" (Rev. 3, 12). It is here that the consciousness of belonging to the Church objectively, becomes the more profound consciousness of participating in the Spirit of the Church.

The "ecclesiastical hierarchy" of Denis the Areopagite rounds off aesthetically this ancient image of the Church and is also responsible for its currency in the Middle Ages. In it, the official hierarchy is incorporated into this comprehensive scheme and interpreted accordingly. The sharp antithesis between the perfect and those on the way to perfection is toned down and reconciled by means of a third, intermediate stage of those who, themselves the object of mediation, begin already to act as mediators. The main import of the word "hierarchy" is drawn from the primitive Christian interpretation of the Church in terms of love; its neo-Platonic guise is purely external. Primarily, it signifies the inner hierarchy of sanctity, to which the official hierarchy is subjoined in a secondary sense. Nonetheless, the love inherent in the Church is itself present impersonally in the office, in accordance with the essential character of Christian love (as a participation in the heavenly hierarchy of the divine love itself).

This image of the Church, in the Middle Ages, came to be centered on Mary, and in this way its inmost truth was brought out. Previously, the "stainlessness" of the holy Church, viewed empirically, could be considered only as an ideal to which she approximated. The apostles were held to be preëminently the core of the actual Church "without spot or wrinkle"; *"Ipsi [apostoli] enim sunt non habentes maculam vel rugam aut aliquid hujusmodi, vera ecclesia"* (Origin). To them were added their successors, the martyrs, and, after the time of Origen, the holy doctors, as evidenced by Bede: "Through the word and example of the holy doctors, the whole structure of the Church, according to Bede, is held together. To them is entrusted the care of the Church, and there is no doubt at all that their firmness is not to be shaken. . . . In the heart of the saints, therefore, the one, true doctrine of the Church is constantly assured; in the works of the saints, the virtue of the Church is ever resplendent and beautiful." Bede was aware of the weaknesses of the empirical Church, those even of its holiest members, and spoke, therefore, as though the Church's stainlessness were a matter of approximation: the Church is realized insofar as sanctity and love are realized: complete sanctity and love, which constitute the "form" of the Church, are, then, to be found in the Head alone.

This opens up three different ways of approach. The Church's sanctity can be held (in the context, for instance, of the Song of Songs or of the Letter to the Ephesians) as an "idea" laid up in heaven above the present reality and informing it. Or else it is seen (and this is closely connected with the first) in the indestructible character of the hierarchical and sacramental structure set up by Christ, thus, in practice, settling the question of a subject of the Church. Or finally, it is centered on Mary's immaculate conception as its personal fixed point. According to this view, Mary stands, as the universal womb bearing progeny, behind the sanctity of the apostles, and great significance is given to her presence with the apostles at Pentecost and receiving the Spirit, so that she is, in a very real sense, able to communicate her Christian wisdom to the apostolic Church. Thus, as Bede tells us, "Philip of Harveng never tires of extolling the maternal activity of Mary in the first ages of the Church, bringing forth the apostles, as if bearing them, out of the darkness of ignorance, bringing them up and forming them, and, as the mother of all, presiding over them, and, through her constancy in faith, calling the vacillating disciples to order." This somewhat external, imaginative presentation gives place to a more interior one in German mysticism, which brings out the idea of the essential fecundity and apostolic character of love (even—and especially —of silent, contemplative love), and so attains to a far deeper comprehension of Mary's role as mediatrix of grace. She is seen as spreading her protective cloak over the whole of Christendom, and making some part of her stainlessness flow out over the bride, the Church. Philip's "education of the apostles" by Mary, which, it is true, has been taken as referring to the sphere of love and fidelity rather than to that of their office, now makes way for the idea of a sheltering of the whole official side of the Church in Mary's maternal womb, which bears, brings forth, and silently represents it. It is significant, however, that even at the beginning of the thirteenth century, John of Pecham saw the Church's unity wholly in terms of love and holiness, into which even the unity of obedience to the hierarchy was integrated. For him, Church unity is (1) unity of love, by which all are one heart and one soul; (2) unity of divinization (that is, of grace), which makes all members of the one Christ; (3) unity of ecclesiastical communion in faith and the sacraments; (4) unity of the hierarchical connection, to which belong the common obedience and also the unity of the apostolic succession from Christ; and, (5) unity of common sentiments (unanimity).

This whole system of ecclesiology, centered on the strongly dynamic idea of love in the Church, ascending and descending, bearing and being borne, and with its organic completion in Mary's immaculate conception, suffered a contraction as a result of the predestination taught by Augustine in his later years. According to Augustine, the final separation spoken of in St. John's letter is something close at hand, definite and tangible: the proper Church (of those who really love) is now explained as or hardened into the "Church of the predestined," and the improper Church (of those in mortal sin within the Church) similarly as the mass of the damned. It is not that Augustine had any thought of empirically determining this final separation; but the line separating, once and for all, the "two kingdoms," ran hidden beneath the earthly frontier between Church and non-Church, though not simply coincident with it. According to John, one did not pray for the reprobate; even Christ on the cross, according to Thomas, could not pray for them. Bearing others in love has certain bounds, even though, for the time being, not verifiable. The fruitfulness of love is not simply infinite. The Church of the elect shuts herself up within herself, and as a result the dark shadows cast a gloom over Christendom from Augustine to Gottschalk and Calvin, disturb men over the question of their own personal salvation. And, with all this, Augustine in his anti-Pelagianism, sees sin present everywhere. The Church's stainlessness is eschatological, and, for the present, is wholly withdrawn into its divine Head. In him, through him, the body is freed from sin. For Augustine, the central image is that of the Head and the body—that of the bride and bridegroom is merely explanatory of this. Just as we speak of a distinct closed period of Church history ending with Constantine, so we may also speak of a closed Augustinian period in ecclesiology (which, though quite different, is nevertheless connected with it below the surface); both of these are now beginning to open up.

The image of the Church, that of dynamic love bearing and being borne (which in its totality is borne by Christ, by God), an image which sees in the Church all gradations of holiness from the highest, most unsullied sanctity of Mary to the very brink of damnation, in fact even beyond it, in the case of the gravely sinful who are yet, in some way, members of the Church

—this image is the justification of these two statements: that the Church, the more "properly" she is the Church, the more stainless, the more conformed to Christ she is, the more Marial, and that she still remains the Church even in the sinner, since he has some velleity and is being borne by the suffering members of the Church, deficient and estranged though it be, and as struggling and in course of conversion. The Church, at her core, remains unspotted and a pure bride. In this, she is distinguished from the synagogue, which, according to the prophets, can become a brazen harlot. There is a certain continuity between the old and the new covenant in that the Church, in her ("improper" but "true" members) sins and falls, and the words of the prophets never cease to apply to us as members of the Church.

This is, in fact, the image of the Church already adopted once one takes seriously the question "Who is the Church?" For the only satisfactory answer is that she consists of real subjects. She is not a *mere* collectivity which, in comparison with the real interconnection between one generation and another of mankind as a whole, always has something fictitious and accidental about it. Real subjects, then, but only such as participate through divine grace in a normative subject and its consciousness. And if this participation is only possible through infused grace, then that in which they participate is divine: the supreme subject demanded by the question posed can only be the divine itself. Mankind gains participation in it through Christ and the sphere which is his (*en Christô*) and which he has prepared as redeemer, namely the Church. Insofar as this sphere is his own, he is her consciousness; and insofar as she makes to him the response of a woman and a bride, she has her supreme, normative subjectivity in Mary. Finally, insofar as the one grace streams through her, this grace makes all spirits, in all their personal varieties of missions and spiritual ways, converge in a single consciousness, opening in Mary to Christ, and through Christ to the Holy Spirit of the three-personal God, who in the beginning overshadowed Mary, and, since Easter and Pentecost, dwells in the Church.

152

This image of the Church also gives a convincing sense to the "myth" of the Church fallen from heaven for whose sake Christ leaves the Father and the heavenly Jerusalem, the mother, in order to go in search of her on earth, and to form with her one flesh. For, in fact, the subject estranged from God, namely, the man Adam and, in him, mankind, is really fallen from paradise, and gone into an alien place far from God. Adamic humanity, and none other, was what the redeemer went to seek. It alone was the subject out of which he willed to form his pure Church. This humanity was, in God's predetermination ideally, and in the first parents, really holy and unstained. Its turning away from God, which could not be put right by man, its banishment to a bodily state subject to the passions and death, likened by Ignatius to an existence in prison among wild beasts, are quite enough justification, on biblical grounds, for the core of the apparent myth. But the return home is achieved, not by a gnostic form of spiritualization, but by the transformation of the flesh estranged from God through the sacrificial fire of the cross, in the mystery of the "one" sacrificed flesh of man and woman, Christ and Church.

6. A UNITY OF UNITIES

This brings us to one last element in the solution of the problem which still remains to be clarified. We found ourselves unable to accede to the view that the Church formally consists only in sacramental grace imparting the form of Christ, and that the human persons taken up into her constitute only the material aspect. That would be to overlook the essential aim: to make the person a member of the Church. Admittedly, that theory appears to be borne out by the fact that the *Ecclesia* of Christ (in contrast with the holy people of old, which was also a people in the natural order) is an assemblage made up entirely of individuals called out of the world, individuals who must expressly renounce their natural connections so as to be incorporated into a new, heavenly people, whose foundation and unity come wholly from above. The Fathers saw Psalm 45 as prophetic of this: "Hear, O daughter, consider, and incline your ear; forget your people and your father's house; and the king will desire your beauty."

Here the people who must be forgotten are a pagan people; there can be no question of an allusion to the racial community of all men in Adam. Nor does the theologoumenon of the first Adam, who comes from the earth, and the second, whose origin is in heaven (1 Cor. 15, 45 f.), speak of a substitution, but of a redemption in time, in which the second Adam presupposes the first, in order (as the context shows, which deals with the resurrection) not to discard him, but to perfect him by his transformation. "Just as we have borne the image of the man of dust [Adam], we shall also bear [by our resurrection] the image of the man of heaven" (*ibid.*, 49). ". . . we sigh with anxiety; not that we would be unclothed, but that we would be further clothed" (2 Cor. 5, 4). For that reason, the Son took flesh from the generation of Adam, and for the same reason the Fathers, in particular Ambrose, saw the formation of the hypostatic union as the real and primordial marriage union, that of God with the whole of mankind: "*At vero postquam Dominus in corpus hoc veniens contubernium divinitatis et corporis . . . sociavit, tunc toto orbe diffusus corporibus humanis vitae celestis usus inolevit.*" This passage, representative of many, especially from the Greek Fathers, shows that the marriage of Christ and the Church is only to be interpreted against the background of an, as it were, fundamental marriage with mankind as a whole. This being so, the encounter of the "unity from above" with the "unity from below" cannot de without significance for the formation of the Church's unity as well. The unity from below is characterized for the Redeemer as the unity of the *massa damnata* tainted with original sin; and the unity from above—God in Christ in the Church—envisages as the ultimate subject of the gift, not individuals taken up out of the *massa damnata,* but nothing less than mankind. It is for this that Christ made satisfaction on the cross; to say otherwise would be Jansenism.

If this is fundamentally correct, then the next question still remains difficult: that of the significance to be attributed to the unity of mankind in relation to that of the Church. Athwart this question lies the freedom of the divine choice and the divine judgment, and it is impossible to work out a systematization on the lines of Origen and Gregory of Nyssa. Nevertheless, the old allegory—older than the Alexandrians—of the one lost sheep sought out by the shepherd and brought home can rightly be applied to mankind. And, basically, the Fathers meant nothing else when they spoke of Christ coming down to earth to bring home his fallen bride. One can only say, then, that the Church represents mankind, stands to it in a necessary, dynamic relationship, even if this cannot be clearly elucidated. We come to our closest understanding of it when we see the Church as the body of Christ, the body he joins to himself to carry out his work of redemption in the world and in mankind, when we consider the Church's "co-redemptive" function—on its own plant—and, in it, her role of mediatrix to the world. Then the whole range of the Church between those who bear and those who are borne, or between the perfect, the advancing, and the beginners, would be no cosmos closed in on itself, but, in its totality something instrumental. To be in the Church would be tantamount to an assignment however inchoate or rudimentary, in the work of the redemption of the world.

Unless one sees the whole matter in this light, the *gratia perficit naturam* is not allowed full scope, and *natura* means merely the individual persons representative of human nature, and not the latter's real totality. Nor would it be metaphysically possible —unless one were to follow a Platonist conception of man—to made a complete disjunction between person and race, so that, if one section of mankind were redeemed and brought into the new unity of the Church, and the other failed to be so transplanted, the original unity which God created, and whose reëstablishment he had in mind (Eph. 1, 10), would still be unimpaired. But as it is, we see the supernatural unity framed on the lines of the natural, the latter being taken up into the former, admittedly in such a way that, in this aeon, the unity

155

of the two unities retains a historical, discriminatory, and representative character as the "struggling Church" of Jesus Christ, as a positive institution equipped to bear witness inwardly and outwardly to the reconciliation of the world achieved in principle, to its redemption still awaited at the end of time. Then the Church's consciousness has really something to do with mankind's consciousness: knowing that mankind is envisaged in God's plan, she can know herself (in the humble awareness of her election) as representative of mankind before God, in faith, prayer, and sacrifice, in hope for all, and still more in love for all. For Christ died for all, and the Father loved all so much as to give his only-begotten Son for them; and Christian love must see in all men those redeemed by Christ, potentially and perhaps actually members of his body.

It is through the Church that God and man encounter one another; and the Church's consciousness cannot be, in any way, closed in and bounded; it is open on both sides, to God and to man. Yet it cannot simply be restricted to being this open center, for we must take account of the nuptial simile, which, in its full sense, is a simile of movement (man going to woman in procreation, woman turning to man in giving him back the perfected offspring). There is no such thing as a Church consciousness simply contrasted with Christ, for the Church, bride as she is, is also his body, informed by the consciousness of the Head; and inasmuch as she has her own existence, she stands open to him, to serve as handmaid. In fact, even this mystery, this movement, cannot be ultimate, since Christ cannot be divorced from the Trinity and that which passes over from him to the Church, in the depths of their intimacy, is the entire Trinitarian life in course of communication.

The Letter to the Ephesians gives us the stages of this unity: ". . . eager to maintain the unity of the Spirit in the bond of peace. There is one body and one Spirit, just as you were called to the one hope that belongs to your call, one Lord, one faith, one baptism, one God and Father of us all, who is above all and through all and in all" (4 3–6). The unity founded, and therefore to be lived, in faith and love is, in the first place, the unity of the "Lord," in whom Christians are "one body," indeed precisely as the epistle to the Galatians says, "one" (3, 28). But, since "the Lord is the Spirit" (2 Cor. 3, 17), and his words are "spirit and life" and "the flesh is of no avail" (Jn. 6, 63), consequently "one body" implies "one Spirit," and this body-spirit is the sacramental form of the Church, to which belongs the "one faith" (as certified formula and infinite content) and the "one baptism" (as rite and infinite efficacy). But this infiniteness of the Spirit is the presence of the Trinitarian God in the Church-body, and therefore, the ultimate and highest orientation to the Father of the work effected by the Son and the Spirit. To him is directed the "one hope that belongs to your call," so that the Church may be not only the fullness of Christ, but also the fullness of the triune God pouring himself out into creation, as Tertullian so boldly says: *"Ubi tres, id est Pater et Filius et Spiritus Sanctus, ibi Ecclesia, quae trium corpus est."*

This should prepare the way for a final word on the Church as bride. If the Church is to be unalterably a unity (with the bridegroom Christ) in contradistinction to him, and if she is thus representative of the opposition of mankind as a whole (as creature) to God (as Creator), then the opposition of God and creature in her will be sublimated, overcome, and fulfilled by being merged in the opposition within the Trinity that accompanies the identity.

7. TRINITY, INCARNATION, CHURCH

We return now to the question of the nuptial union between Christ and the Church, in which she becomes not only "one body," but also, as has been said above, "one Spirit." For Christ, who made over his body to the Church before the passion, breathed his Spirit into her at Easter. If one considers the image, which Paul calls a "great mystery" (Eph. 5, 32), in the light of this very fulfillment, then we find it elucidated from above, while it, in turn, illuminates the mystery of the Church.

The marriage union presupposes three things: (1) two persons, who, even in the union, remain unmixedly persons, and only so are in a condition to experience physical union as a rapturous encounter of their spirits or persons; (2) a physical union of such a kind as to make them both truly "one flesh," as is shown externally by the result, the child, in whom the share of both is not only physically, but metaphysically, indistinguishable; (3) a physical opposition of the sexes which represents the opposition of the spiritual persons in the bodily sphere, and, at the same time makes possible their union in one flesh, this irreducible opposition being the basis of the irrefragable union.

By uniting these three, man gives the real proof of his being the center and crown of creation. Here nature (the material, subhuman, vital creation) and spirit (superhuman, angelic essence) come together and complete one another in a creative act. For procreation and birth, in the subhuman sphere, presuppose imperfect individuation, the immersion of the individuals in a common ocean of biological life, and it is only as representing this that they fulfill the act of reproduction, which is of necessity sealed by their incomplete individuation in death.

The angelic spirit, on the other hand, has a monadic structure, and does not reproduce itself. However profound and fruitful the mutual encounter of angels may be held to be, they certainly have no part in the animal experience of rapt submission to the invasion of the life-force, whether specific or generic.

But how man is able to conjoin the two must be the most profound mystery of the natural order: the encounter of spirit with spirit under the sign of bodily coalescence on the one hand, and, on the other, a bodily union whose rapture and fruitfulness is, as it were, a natural sacramental sign and indication of spiritual union—for the fruit is, beyond anything that might be expected, not only a new individuation of universal life, but incomprehensibly, a new person. Undoubtedly, the theory of creationism, taken by itself or superficially, fails to do justice to the power of human coition, since it must certainly exceed that of the animals, and is conjoined with the divine primary cause, without which the coming into being of a person would be inexplicable. The Thomist theory of a succession of forms, each higher than the preceding, during the development of the embryo, though very ingenious, possibly minimizes the human share too much, and unduly splits up the spiritual, animal, vegetative soul in *fieri* (not in *esse*). However this may be, it is certain that the child is a product, not only of husband and wife, but also of earth and heaven. And it is man's incomprehensible, irrefragable glory that in marriage (which biologically bears, even for him, the germ of death) he can make a mutual and personal asseveration of immortality, of a love, that is, which precisely because it can reproduce and die, knows itself immortal. Truly, for him the infinite emerges from the finite, like foam on a troubled sea.

Paul, however, calls this a great mystery in relation to Christ and the Church. The lines leading up from the natural to the supernatural mystery, which is a mystery of faith, can still only be drawn tentatively and by way of suggestions. The most difficult line is the first: marriage requires two persons. We have attempted to give some intimation of the personality of the Church. We could not hypostasize the Church, nor did we wish to see her as a mere collectivity. Neither is there a collective person resulting from the merging of the individual persons. There is absolutely no analogy for the reality which revelation calls the bride of Christ; and since God's Trinitarian consciousness in Christ is embedded in her to make her a bride, an individual subject, this subject-being is itself a mystery of faith. We attempted to clarify it through the encounter of God's unity with mankind's, an encounter which raises the latter unity (which consists of innumerable persons) to a participation in the three-personal Spirit-unity of God; an encounter, however, which is fulfilled in history and in the event involving the incarnate God and the persons of the elect, who have already received, and mirror forth, the Spirit of Christ and the Trinity. It is only when God sees himself in the mirror of the creature that there has been response to him and an encounter with him.

But he can only see himself in a living mirror, in which the character of man as created in the divine image is stamped with the seal of grace, and so becomes a part of the total and adequate response. This sublime elevation of man as an ever-personal being, yet with a sexual role, is the place of the unity of the bride.

The second element, that the bride is here the very body of the man Christ, is less difficult to understand. It is true that we are again confronted with a mystery which cannot be educidated: that of the Eucharist, which must be presupposed in order to understand the real bodily character of the bride as something supernatural, imparted by Christ. But Christ is a real man, and as such, he also touches the biological plane and that of sub-personal individuation; and were it not for his union with the Church on this level also, the marriage simile could not be sustained. Nonetheless, the emphasis in the union is not on the first Adam, the man of dust—on the *bios*—but on the second Adam, the man of heaven—on the *Logos* and the *pneuma*. Of man it was said: " 'The two shall become one.' But he who is united to the Lord becomes one spirit with him" (1 Cor. 6, 16–17). Here, the flesh alone is of no avail; here the bare sacrament also is of no avail: it is only the Spirit, placed by the Lord in flesh and sacrament, and received by faith, that makes the fleshly sacramental bridge capable of bearing its load. Yet even the marriage symbol pointed in this direction, and was therefore a "great mystery." The fleshly element was already seen as a "sacrament" of personal encounter, but only fully so when marriage between Christians became a true sacrament, and was understood in light of the mystery of the union consummated by Christ and his Church. Nevertheless, in the following chapter (1 Cor. 7), Paul sets virginity above marriage, since that is the way in which the believer, going beyond the earthly simile, gives himself directly (from without the center of the Church, as person) to the Lord, nuptially, and is fused nuptially with him. This is certainly true in the *pneuma*, but also in the mystery of the "one flesh" which Christ and the Church form

160

together. Virginity outside the Church can only be a negative and ascetic concept, but within the Church it is the pure way of participating in the mystery of flesh and spirit of the God-man that is fulfilled in the Eucharist, cross, and resurrection.

The third element, the mystery of the opposition, has already been presented in its Christological setting. The Church is not, purely and simply, Christ. She is not hypostatically united to God who dwells in her. In this opposition, therefore, she is receptive to her Head, and so has a feminine role. She is Marial, in the sense already explained. In this consists the fulfillment of the creaturely opposition that underlies the mystery of love and fecundity in the bodily sphere, a fulfillment that is only to be derived from the highest sphere, that of the Trinitarian opposition of Persons in identity of nature. It is comprehensible that the seal of identity should be imprinted from above on the oppositions that arise in salvation history: thus, too, the opposition between Christ as bridegroom, and the Church as bride, is subsumed in the identity of the one Christ, Head and body, who, as *Christus totus,* is for Augustine "one person," and for Paul the "one" (see Gal. 3, 28). This seal of identity imprints itself right through the unity Christ-Church until it reaches that most fundamental opposition which rejects identity, because in it the dissimilarity is ever greater than the similarity—the opposition, that is, of God and creature. In the hypostatic union (and its imperfect participation in the Church), even this irreducible abbyss, without being eliminated, is bridged and tunneled by the power of God's love.

In these three points, then, marriage is a symbol of the redemption. If the first, the irreducibility of the subjects, were lacking to redemption, then instead of redemption by grace, we should have a pantheism that eliminates the creature. If the second, the one flesh as sacrament of the one spirit, were lacking, then the unity would not be truly brought about, and we should remain with that juridical conception which is generally (whether rightly or not) laid to the charge of Protestantism. If the third, the relative opposition of the sexes, were lacking, we should lapse into a kind of religious homosexuality, in which the creature would relate himself to God in a masculine fashion, a sin of which non-Christian mysticism is guilty in a subtle way, as is, in a less subtle way, religious magic, whose perverse encroachment on God himself (appearing in angelic form) is depicted in the story of Sodom and its destruction. Consequently, a typical pagan utterance like that cited by Paul in Athens ("we are indeed his offspring"— Acts 17, 28), can really be adduced only in a marginal sense and for purposes of illustration. With God there can be no union of the same sex, but only a feminine dependence on God, as taught by Paul and Augustine: no taking, but only a being taken. As the individual believer lets himself be taken by God, becoming a handmaid of the Lord, so the Church awakens in him and, in feminine fashion, reflects the Spirit of the Lord. It is both the lowliness and glory of woman to be obliged and to be able to receive in this way. But since we are sinners, this humility must be instilled into us by humiliation: "But we have this treasure in earthen vessels, to show that the transcendent power belongs to God and not to us" (2 Cor. 4, 7).

If we consider the marriage act not so much from the angle of the partners as from that of the offspring, it can be seen to involve three elements, in ascending gradation, all of which are necessary for the production of offspring: a material element— seed; a biological element—life; and a personal element—immortal spirit. Though these elements are easily distinguishable in the abstract, the distinction is very difficult when it comes to the actual sources of the operation. With animals, and even with plants, the material element, the seed, itself contains the life which is to be built up, but, at the same time, this life is an offshoot of the total life of the species, in fact of cosmic life in general. With man, on the other hand, since a spiritual person is produced, the "world-soul" is not the only active agent—God, personal and creative, is himself active.

The Church likewise originates from a "seed," which is the body and blood of Christ delivering himself to death for the life of the world. But the "life" by which he is a living being is his "Spirit," which, as was shown, must be both divine and human spirit: the spirit which was breathed forth on the cross with water and blood, and sent back to the Father, and which is, therefore, inseparable from the Holy Spirit whom the risen Christ breathed on his Church (Jn. 20) and sent down upon the Church after the ascension, when he forms once more a joint principle of spiration with the Father, as a Spirit at once Trinitarian and Christological in union with the Father. In this community of spiration, which involves the participation of the Father in the whole work of building up the Church, we see the third element in the process, the coöperation of God the Creator.

For the Church to come into being, a productive act is required, and this extends from the man dying on the cross (who lets body and spirit and person flow out of himself so fully that he is himself all outpouring and seed, that the Creator dissolves in the creation the priest in the sacrifice)—extends through the communication of his own both human and divine spirit into the very mysteries of the generation and spiration within the Trinity. Here indeed the person is not distinguished from the life flow in which the Father is active generation, the Son passive generation, where being Son and being Word of the Father are not distinguishable, and breathing forth and being breathed forth are identical as one event, though they involve the eternal relative opposition of the Spirit to Father and Son, whose identical love is the Spirit.

Thus it is evident that the self-outpouring in death and resurrection of God's incarnate Word into the Church is truly the pouring forth of the Trinitarian life externally. The virginal man Christ is wholly (as Hamann most profoundly divined) the generative organ (*instrumentum conjunctum*) of the eternally generating Godhead, and the central organ in that it belongs to him alone to make himself (in the Eucharist) a seed and, at the same time—beyond any analogy with the way in which man and the Creator coöperate—to pour out his Spirit into what is produced, through his joint spiration with God the Father.

163

At this point, we must mark precisely the distinction between creation in nature and supernature on the one hand, and between generation in nature and supernature on the other. Natural generation presupposes the sexual partnership, but the female partner, the Church, that is to originate from Christ, is not yet in existence. It must first of all come into being by generation through the cross, resurrection, and ascension. There is eros when the love which generates can *pre*suppose the natural *pre*presence of the one loved (in its difference as in its similarity of nature); *agapē,* on the other hand, creates out of complete *self*lessness that which is to be loved. But the Son's creation of the Church is not the same thing as the Father's creation of the world, for it presupposes the latter and fulfills it in grace. It is, therefore, on the level of "nature" analogous to eros between the sexes, but on the level of "supernature" analogous to the Father's act of creation, since grace can never develop out of nature. On the level of nature, the subject humanity is presupposed, as the individual humanity of the separate persons no less than as the collective reality and unity of all the individuals descended from Adam and Eve. Into this natural unity is poured the seed of the dead and risen Word of God. But the analogy with nature seems preserved through Christ's relationship to Mary, in which the purely natural unity raised to a real feminine partnership in Mary's *fiat,* comprising all the inchoate acts of assent and faith of the old Zion as well as of Peter representing the Church and of the other apostles and disciples, represents the true matrix of the Church to be brought forth. If we bear this in mind, it becomes almost palpably evident how Mary (and, conjoined with her, the entire supernatural reality of faith in the world around Christ) is both the prerequisite and womb of the coming Church as well as being herself the Church generated, since Mary's preredemption and the faith of the old covenant also refer back to the generative redemptive act of Christ. The Church as the female partner is both produced and presupposed in the generative act of Christ. Otherwise, this would not be both divine and human.

This being so, the feminine character of the Church as a subject is, moreover, posited and presupposed; and it is not only presupposed in the sense that nature (created humanity collective and personal) is presupposed as the subject of attribution, to which the grace of rebirth can be given, but also, as implied by the old covenant, Mary and the Church of those who believe and love—which involve a believing subject informed by grace. But this inchoate subject, the Church, is fulfilled only in the mystery of the Holy Spirit, who is embedded in her as her inmost ground, and who can therefore constitute it in its perfected state because he is a divine Person precisely *as* testifying to the eternal opposition of the persons. In virtue of this divine *coincidentia oppositorum,* he is the founder and foundation of the "other," the bride—who, yet, is as such the "one," the body—and out of the oneness of the "Spirit of Christ" creates in all believers the "opposition of being" resulting from the same Spirit of Christ. Simultaneously, then, he makes the One out of the Other (that is, he brings back the creation, which as regards God is the Other, into the divine law of life, and subordinates to it this otherness), and at the same time makes the Other out of the One (that is, from the hypostatic union of Christ he brings forth the double subject Christ-Church). Thus the return of the creature into God becomes simultaneously the outgoing of the divine life, which, entering into the creature, draws it into the eternal opposition of the persons in love and through love.

4.

THE CHURCH AND ISRAEL

THE dissensions which accompany the foundation of anything new are so destructive that the harm they have done seems
irreparable. Catholics and Protestants at first used harsh and violent language about one another, until, growing tired, they gave
it up. Now they are slowly beginning to look upon the cleavage
as unnecessary, and tentatively to resume communication—but
the harm caused by that strife within Christianity is trifling compared with the dissensions and divison brought about by the
sword which Christ set up in the midst of his earthly kingdom,
the sword spoken of in the Bible, which pierced his own and his
mother's heart, and also the heart of the Jew called to be the
apostle of the Gentiles, who confessed to having "such great
sadness and continual sorrow in his heart" that he could wish
to be anathema to Christ if that would but take away the re-
proach from his people.

Now, if the dialogue between Jews and Christians, almost,
though not entirely in abeyance for a thousand years, is to be
resumed, one thing is clear: it must be resumed at the very core,
the pulsating heart, of the Bible. Furthermore, those who, in
fact, completed the cleavage of going further (although, in their
own view, guiltless), should suffer more on its account than
those who have remained as they were. There is an element of
harshness and abruptness in the New Testament situation that
no dialogue can mitigate, unless it is to become quite unreal.

166

The passage of two thousand years has not altered this situation by bringing a synthesis nearer; nor can one ever hope to reach agreement beyond the cross and the resurrection as it were, on a purely human level. Nothing can alter the fact that Jesus left the Jews to themselves, that the apostles, after their initial attempt at a dialogue, systematically did likewise. Is his failure with the people of Israel a deficit impossible to repair, a congenital defect, so to speak, of his religion? And a still more searching question: Has not, perhaps, the anti-Jewish front of all the Gospels and the apostolic writings been responsible for the frightful anti-Semitism running through the Church's history, which certainly remains a blot on the Church viewed empirically, and also provided Christians in their instinctive hatred with the plausible excuse of theological justification and obedience to the Bible?

We have no qualification, as Christians, to answer these questions; our obligation is to hear God's word and to try to think in obedience to it. All well-intentioned fraternizing between Jews and Christians, all roundtable discussions must, if any result is to accrue, be conducted in the presence of God's word. But this at once tears us apart, since what for us is God's word, the New Testament, and especially Romans 9–11, is not such for the Jews. Let us, however, attempt the only course possible for us Christians. Let us speak to our Jewish brothers through the word of God, through Romans 9–11. We shall find that three fundamental theses emerge.

First: *Israel's obduracy enters incontestably into God's plan of salvation in its historical working characterized by election and reprobation.* Now, this implies three things.

1. Paul's statements belong to the theology of history. They are made from the standpoint of the divine way of acting, and so utterly transcend human perspectives of salvation history, as well as the plane of human works. God is the author of the problem, and to him alone belongs its resolution. The uncom-

167

promising harshness with which they are stated, deliberately intended to wound and scandalize, serves solely to bring home to man his incompetence in the whole matter. Has not God the right to choose and to reject, to have mercy and to harden? You object: Why then does he punish? Paul does not answer the objection, but brushes it aside: O man, who art thou that repliest against God? Cannot the potter break up the vessel? Is not the whole Bible, from Moses to Hosea and Isaiah, full of instances of this kind, of the injustice of God? Later, Paul elucidates all that can be elucidated, but only to end in praise of the "unsearchable counsels and unfathomable ways" of God. Everything up to the very end remains his plan, his execution, his mystery. Whoever intervenes with good advice, like Peter, dissuading the Lord from his passion, is the adversary, Satan, and comes under God's displeasure.

2. The whole point at issue is clearly the obduracy which is the sign of God's rejection. The expressions are heaped up: "blindness," "hardness," "obduracy," "deafness," "snare," "trap," "stumbling," and finally, "rejection." The problem is not whether Israel is to blame for this fate, which St. Paul affirms expressly and incontrovertibly, and demonstrates at length: the guilt lies on those who put works in the place of faith, the tangible results of what is fleshly and earthly in the place of being led by the promise and the Spirit. But this is only a sort of parenthesis in St. Paul's train of thought. He shows only incidentally that God's rejection was just, which really did not need to be proved. The one important thing here is that Israel's condition is due to a sovereign act of God, infinitely surpassing anything man might have done to bring it about. Human guilt is certainly present within the all-embracing act of God, but it does not determine this act, and this is shown by the fact that it is embraced by the act of election and reconciliation as by that of reprobation and condemnation. God rejects, *because* man is guilty; he also has mercy, *because* man is guilty. The final, decisive *because* rests with God.

3. This twofold action of God's is clearly concerned with history, secular and salvation history. It is the greatest tragedy in the history of Christian theology that this truth should have been so completely ignored. From the time of Augustine, Paul's statements have been taken out of their context in the history of theology, have been applied to individuals, and referred to their eternal salvation or damnation, to heaven and hell. But they are not concerned with this at all. It is true that Paul elucidates the twofold action of God with reference to various personalities representative of the people, to Isaac and Ishmael, Jacob and Esau, Moses and Pharaoh; but are we to conclude that Ishmael Esau, and Pharaoh are eternally damned? More especially since the idea of eternal hell can only be a New Testament one, which presupposes the elimination of that of the common Hades or Sheol. The theology of predestination which prevailed from St. Augustine throughout the Middle Ages and on to Luther and Calvin—whether well-founded or not—can most certainly not appeal to the great Pauline passage on God's twofold action in salvation history. So far is this from it that, as Karl Barth so convincingly shows in his *Church Dogmatics,* even the New Testament statements on individual reprobation and election should be read in the light of these social statements on world history and salvation history, and not vice versa. But we are not for the moment concerned with this, only with the fact that God's total and indivisible, if two-sided action upon mankind is concerned with its salvation, expressing, in both aspects, the divine economy of salvation.

Second: *The reprobation of Israel serves to the election of the Gentiles who, as the elect, are the spiritual Israel and have their lasting roots fixed in the old Israel.* Using this theodicy of history, Paul illuminates the mystery of the dual nature of God's action, without thereby depriving it of its character, its mystery, or making it comprehensible, after the manner of Hegel, in terms of a philosophy of history. Once more, three things are implied:

1. Israel's reprobation serves to the election of the Gentiles: this statement is made with the utmost clarity. Certainly, Israel is not to blame for not having believed in God. It is not this, however, that affects the Gentiles, but solely the interim state of blindness to which God has destined Israel in her guilt, a state which allows those formerly blind to see, those formerly deaf to hear the word proclaimed. Never are the elect granted any sort of right over those blinded, no spiritual right either to lord it over them in their humiliation, no right to mockery, revenge, persecution, anti-Semitism. The shadow cast over Israel by God comes from God. It is the shadow of God himself, given solely as a mirror for those entered into the light, to make them realize the darkness from which they themselves came, and into which they fall back if they "puff themselves up"; to show them that they must ascribe their election solely to grace; and, finally, to illustrate the indissoluble union and destiny binding those in darkness and those in the light. Indeed, St. Paul goes so far as to say that the Gentiles owe their "engrafting" to the fact of the Jews being "cut off," and so to God's action on them, not to their own sinful action, their self-blinding, which is, indeed, included in the former. This brings those rejected and cut off into a unique relationship to the Messiah, who for the world's redemption was "made sin" by God: as we Christians cannot look on him without seeing the wounds caused by our sins—since, innocent, he bore them for us—so guilty Israel, according to Paul, suffers for the world's redemption, and in the burden laid on Israel that assumed by us is clearly incorporated. And so anyone who strikes Israel strikes the Messiah, who, as God's suffering servant, gathers up in himself all the afflictions of God's servant, Israel.

2. The election, however, that for a time is taken away from Israel in order that the Gentiles may be incorporated, is the same as the old, unique election of mankind in Abraham, Isaac, and Jacob, into which the universality of peoples is now in-

170

corporated. Here the Jews and the Gentiles can be seen as in-
extricably intertwined, in so subtle a way as to suggest God's
direct leading. Where Israel is concerned, this means that it was,
from the outset, a function of the final election of the Gentiles
—so much so, in fact, that it was not the fleshly Israel that came
first in God's plan, in order to be the promise of a subsequent
spiritual Israel, but, as Paul shows in detail, the fleshly Israel
which was, from the first, based upon the spiritual. Fleshly
generation is the work of man, but Isaac's generation was itself
a function of the spiritual promise of God to a sterile couple,
and of Abraham's spiritual faith in that promise. This recurring
doctrine of Paul occurs here significantly. The same is true,
later, of the birth of the twin brothers, where the natural order
is reversed—and equally throughout the whole destiny of the
people, of which only a remnant attains the promise, while the
greater part comes to grief in the desert, in exile and diaspora.
Their collapse is the collapse of the fleshly Israel: the remnant
is the distillation and quintessence of the spiritual Israel, which
was intended from the very beginning. From this it follows that
the dialectic of election and reprobation did not take place only
between synagogue and Church, but was present already within
Judaism and the Law: the Church of the Gentiles only participates therein as fulfilling it, and, henceforth, as the spiritual
Israel, forming a single figure together.

This must, therefore, also be considered in relation to the
Church, for if the universal Church is the fulfillment of the
promise made to Abraham, she is, in fact, to use Paul's image,
grafted onto the olive tree, whose own branches lie beside it, cut
off in order that the wild branches may be inserted. "If some of
the branches be broken, and you, being a wild olive, are en-
grafted in them and made partaker of the root and sap of the
olive tree, boast not against the branches. But if you boast, consider: you do not bear the root, but the root bears you." What
is striking about this crucial passage is that it makes no mention
of Christ, who is on every other occasion described as the foundation, the vine from which the branches flourish and are fruit-

ful. Where is Christ to be found in this image, which only illustrates the relation between promise and fulfillment, Israel and the Church? On both sides, certainly. He is the true fulfillment, the rod from the root of Jesse; and although he was before Abraham came to be, and Abraham for his sake obtained the promise, he is still the true seed of Abraham, the prophet foretold by Moses, the true son of David, the true servant of God described by Isaiah, the true flesh and blood of his Jewish mother Mary. According to the flesh, he is an Israelite, which means that he is also the flower and fruit of the entire Israelite faith, hope, love, prayer, and suffering. Jesus is at once a Jew and Son of the Father: he has his enduring roots both in Abraham and in heaven. And the Church which issues from Jesus' life and death, being rooted in him, must likewise have its roots in both.

3. Paul adds two further qualifications: he says that what is still visible of Israel, side by side with the Church, consists of severed branches. And yet the Church is not grafted onto a dead, but a living root, from which she draws the sap which he describes as "holy." "If the root is holy, so also are the branches." Consequently, there is something present in the Church of the Gentiles—and this is the crux of the matter—something which is older than herself, in virtue of which she is what she is. This is the ancient, *irrevocable* promise of God to his people. From this, it necessarily follows that if the Jewish promise, transcended so as to refer to the salvation of the whole world, and giving the people a representative character in the process of redemption, if this promise, fulfilled in Christ's sacrifice made in his representative capacity, is present as a living and holy root in and under the Church, then it is evident that the Church, too, participates in the sap of the root, that is to say, in the redemptive destiny of holy Israel in its representative character, the destiny fulfilled in Jesus Christ. The Church, in other words, in spite of her character as light and fulfillment, still shares in

the Judaic and messianic destiny of suffering in her role of representative, and bears a promise that carries her beyond herself, which can only be fulfilled at the end of time. It must be realized that this does not mean that Israel's promise lives on elsewhere than in the Church of Christ. Nor is it said that Israel as, theologically speaking, a historical mission to fulfill in mankind, different from that of the Church, as is constantly alleged. Hypotheses of this sort, whether proposed by Jewish thinkers, by Judaeo-Christian historical theologians, or by Christians like Soloviev (in his celebrated essay *Das Judentum und die christliche Frage*) or Léon Bloy (in *Le Salut par les Juifs*), have a millennialist character: they transfer what belongs to eschatology into the historical future, thus making it a matter of historical progress. This distortion is indeed the one remaining chance open to Jewish ideology, with whose communist or liberal stamp we are familiar. The idea of progress can perhaps be buttressed by a theology of creation, but there is no room for it in a history of grace and salvation understood in a Christian sense. Yet, in spite of all, Israel's promise is not dead. It lives on to the very end, to the moment when the holy root bursts forth, blossoms and bears fruit, in the spiritual Israel of the greatest of the sons of Abraham. The two destinies, then, lie not alongside but within one another, corresponding to the one, sole promise and fulfillment.

Third: *Israel's rejection, as a factor of salvation history, points to an eschatological salvation common to it and the Church, in which rejection and election are brought into equilibrium.* The intertwining of the two destinies is carried through by Paul to its ultimate consequence.

1. Insofar as Israel's hope has been realized in Jesus Christ, present though hidden in the Church, it has been objectively fulfilled, and for Israel too. But insofar as Israel, for the time being, has been deprived of the perception of this fulfillment (Mt. 23, 38–39; 2 Cor. 3, 15; Rom. 11, 10), and yet cannot

cease to hope in the promise without ceasing to exist, its hope must be the same as that of the Church. Because the Church hopes for the return of Christ who will make the reconciliation of the world by the cross, hitherto hidden, into its manifest redemption in glory, Israel's expectation of salvation is justified both objectively and subjectively, and the sufferings she endures for her own and the world's redemption are to be seen in the same light as this hope, insofar as it is present. Peter, in his sermon in the temple, expressly acknowledged the rightfulness of this hope of the Jews, excusing them on the ground of ignorance for the death of the Messiah, a death which served for the world's redemption. "Repent therefore, and turn again, that your sins may be blotted out, that times of refreshing may come from the presence of the Lord, and that he may send the Christ appointed for you, Jesus, whom heaven must receive until the time for establishing all that God spoke by the mouth of his holy prophets from of old" (Acts 3, 19–21). Paul speaks to the same effect, and with the same unrestricted generality, in regard to the salvation of the chosen people: "And so all Israel should be saved, as it is written: There shall come out of Zion he that shall deliver and shall turn away ungodliness from Jacob. And this is to them my covenant, when I shall take away their sins."

It is no concern of Christians to distinguish in Israel's attitude what is deliberate persistence in defiance and what is a survival and continuance of genuine hope. Their task is, rather, to draw Israel's hope in the darkness into the Christian hope in the light, aware of their responsibility to bear the light on behalf of those in the dark, but also, remembering Paul's warning, in fear of the light, which knows itself to be borne by the darkness (for roots are always in darkness).

2. The destiny of each grows alike in their long waiting for the full and final redemption, and produces a sort of harsh symmetry: "As you also in times past did not believe God, but

now have obtained mercy through their unbelief; so these also now have not believed for your mercy, that they also may obtain mercy." For the Jews, first light, then darkness; for the Christians, first darkness, then light; their roles unchangeable in the economy of salvation in time, and yet, seen from the pinnacle of God's eternity, symmetrical and balanced, and transcending whatever "jealousy" is occasioned, indeed intended, by the one-sidedness of election: "God has included all in unbelief, that he may have mercy on all." Their mutual jealousy over election evaporates in the prison common to all; and finally even the legitimate antinomies are dissolved—antinomies independent of any human antipathy or hatred—and rooted in the true functions pertaining to their respective missions, which allow of no reconciliation of differences on the purely human level, such as the liberal Jews would like. Honor is thus accorded to what is merely human, and, still more, to the religious and theological zeal of Jews and Christian alike. But over and above all, sole honor to the one Redeemer of both: "Who is it that has first given unto him, that he must be repaid? For of him, and through him, and unto him are all things: to him be the glory for ever. Amen."

3. The sap of the living root of Jesse ascends through Jesus Christ out of the old covenant unto the new. God allowed the sap of grace and wisdom to mature and condense in the old covenant for a thousand years, manifesting the process for all times in the sacred Jewish books. If Christ is the transcendent synthesis of the whole, we still need to gaze, again and again, on the parts, if we are not to misunderstand the power of the whole. Whenever the Church forgets the power, the drive, the *kabôd,* the tremendous prophetic insistence of the old covenant, if only for an instant, she falls at once from the height she occupies, her salt becomes tasteless, her image of Christ begins to resemble the Christ of the Pre-Raphaelites. Even when she pays exclusive attention to Paul, and neglects James, the Jew, with his

philosophically stringent demands for the practice of love in the secular sphere and for changes in the social structure, his tirades against the rich, his religion of actions and works, the Jewish element which, in fact, pervades all the Gospels, the Church is no longer universal and catholic. No doubt, there is a permanent Jewish demand on Christendom, which is no other than the enduring demand of the old covenant on the new.

As a result of biblical research, we Christians of today know better than past generations that the Bible is not a book fallen from heaven, mechanically inspired, but that its inspiration developed and came to completion in the heart of the Israel which fought, prayed, and suffered untold pain. We can no longer subscribe to the view of the Fathers, who so strongly felt the transition to the Church as a change in the legitimate ownership of the sacred books. When she received Israel's noblest legacy, the Church obtained not just vegetative sap from the root, but human sap, the lifeblood of Israel, mingled with her high consciousness of mission and the dark depths of sufferings that this mission entailed. Ultimately, they are two chambers of the one heart which beats, which indeed beats on the cross of the world, were the dividing wall was broken down and all hate was overcome in the flesh of the suffering Christ, so that in his person, the two are made one, in the single new man who is our peace (Eph. 2, 14–15).

Year by year, the Church prays on Holy Saturday: "O God, we see your wondrous works of old enlighten even our own day. For the salvation that you bestowed by the power of your right hand upon one nation, as you rescued them from the Egyptian persecution, is now conferred upon all nations by means of the water of regeneration. Grant that the peoples of the whole world may become the descendants of Abraham and share the prerogative of Israel. Through Jesus Christ."